I0819487

The Official American Girl Cookbook

Fancy Food and Cocktails for Grown-Up Fans

Tara McNamara

Illustrated by Jillian Goeler

RUNNING PRESS
PHILADELPHIA

Running Press
Hachette Book Group
1290 Avenue of the Americas
New York, NY 10104
www.runningpress.com
@Running_Press

First Edition: April 2026

Published by Running Press, an imprint of Hachette Book Group, Inc. The Running Press name and logo are trademarks of Hachette Book Group, Inc.

The Hachette Speakers Bureau provides a wide range of authors for speaking events. To find out more, go to www.hachettespeakersbureau.com or email HachetteSpeakers@hbgusa.com.

Running Press books may be purchased in bulk for business, educational, or promotional use. For more information, please contact your local bookseller or the Hachette Book Group Special Markets Department at Special.Markets@hbgusa.com.

The publisher is not responsible for websites (or their content) that are not owned by the publisher.

Print book cover and interior design by Frances J. Soo Ping Chow

Library of Congress Cataloging-in-Publication Data has been applied for.

ISBNs: 978-0-7624-8878-0 (hardcover); 978-0-7624-8879-7 (ebook)

Printed in China

APS

10 9 8 7 6 5 4 3 2 1

Contents

INTRODUCTION

Dolls That Dare

When The American Girls Collection made its debut in 1986, it introduced girls to a new, exciting way of play. The original three characters—patriotic, bespectacled, brunette Molly McIntire; elegant, beautifully bowed Samantha Parkington; and sweet, braided, blonde Kirsten Larson—set hearts afire. Creator Pleasant Rowland had an idea for dolls that were unlike any other at the time—complete with an engaging historical backstory, purposeful wardrobe, and detailed accessories. What started with three dolls and an idea to empower girls turned into a beloved brand that encourages imagination, recognizes individual courage and resilience, and uplifts the uniqueness of all girls.

Pleasant Rowland with Kirsten, Samantha, and Molly (1986).

As The American Girls Collection grew, more characters with historical backgrounds were added and came to be known as the Historical Characters. With the addition of Kaya, Addy Walker, Josefina Montoya, Kit Kittredge, and more, AG expanded its offerings to reflect the experiences, hardships, and triumphs of girls across backgrounds and time. Eventually, American Girl introduced the Girl of the Year and Truly Me dolls to reflect current times, as well as the customizable Create Your Own dolls.

The American Girls Collection created a multitude of avenues that allowed fans to play and connect more with the dolls: books about arts, crafts, fashion, and cooking; magazines that featured paper dolls and stories of other real girls; virtual games where users could "exist" in an American Girl world. Through these offerings and the imagination they fueled, American Girl lovers were inspired to put on AG plays, write music, host AG-themed parties, make new outfits with the Fashion Studio, or take up sewing to create new dresses for their dolls and for themselves.

Whether you strongly associated with a particular Historical Character, were a fan of the *American Girl* magazine, enjoyed diving into the books and stories, or simply loved to flip through the catalog, there was room for everyone to access and enjoy the world of American Girl. Maybe that's why, even as fans have gotten older, the brand is still beloved. If American Girl has taught us anything, it's that girlhood is and always will be something to celebrate.

And the fans who grew up with AG keep this idea close to the heart. Millennials and older Gen Z American Girl fans are now celebrating their birthdays at the American Girl Café, with dolls and with or without children. And sometimes, sans birthdays: the AG adult fans over age twenty-one find there is a thrill in being immersed in childhood while indulging in adult behavior, like setting a girl gathering at the café and drinking Champagne.

With this renaissance, AG adults are creating new ways to let our AG love live on—podcasts, American Girl stop-motion video digital shorts, doll photography, costuming and sewing projects, Halloween costumes, and American Girl–themed parties. AG adults are revealing themselves through skits on *Saturday Night Live* and on female-led talk shows. And now—hello!—a cookbook for us to enjoy American Girl full throttle, as adults!

Many of us ate up the fun of cooking with the dolls and their stories as kids, using the American Girl historically accurate cookbooks so we could make cornbread like Addy and bizcochitos like Josefina and bask in the joy of making our Kirsten dreams come true by baking St. Lucia buns (admit it, you braided your hair for that one). This cookbook is a little different—it's a celebration of your childhood while recognizing your adulthood.

The Official American Girl Cookbook: Fancy Food and Cocktails for Grown-Up Fans provides a fun and delicious exploration of new recipes to continue that exciting, nostalgic, happy, warm, and fuzzy joy of dining with your doll at your own home, as an adult. Whether dining with your American Girl doll or American Girl friends, chapters serve up suggestions for girl gatherings, with recipes for main and side dishes, light bites, and cocktails and mocktails that connect to the Historical Characters or Girls of the Year. Whether you're watching a big game, getting ready for a concert, or celebrating a birthday, American Girl is here to feed your soul, at any age. Cheers!

See me
HEAR ME
know
Me

Sip Tips

Here is how to ensure your cocktails look as good as they taste!

Simple Syrup

Most of our drink recipes call for simple syrup. Simple syrup provides the basis for various creative flavorings. True to its name, it is simple to make—and with such little effort and expense, it's just as easy to experiment with different herbs, fruits, and flowers to concoct your own signature taste. Known for balancing the taste of alcohol, it can also add sweetness to nonalcoholic beverages, like tea and lemonade.

INGREDIENTS

1 cup water

1 cup sugar

RECIPE STEPS

1. Boil water in a medium saucepan over medium heat.
2. Add sugar, stirring frequently until dissolved. Bring back to a boil.
3. Take off heat.
4. Once cooled, the syrup is ready to use.
5. Refrigerate for up to one month in an airtight container.

To infuse a flavor into the syrup, add a handful of the fruit, spice, or herb of choice to the pot. For example, for rosemary, add two sprigs. For cinnamon, add four sticks. For blueberries, add 1 cup. When the water boils, turn the temperature down to a simmer for 10 minutes. Let it cool. Strain out the solids and pour the syrup into an airtight container.

How to Rim a Glass

Rims add extra zing to the flavor of a drink and make a cocktail look more inviting. Salt for a margarita, tajin for a spicy drink, or sugar for a lemon drop are common examples. Creating a rim isn't hard but requires a little finesse. Simply, you wet the rim and then add the seasoning around the edge.

To wet the rim, citrus fruits—like lime, lemon, or orange—are fantastic for taste and ease. Cut into a slice of lime or orange and rub around the top of the glass.

For a sweet rim, like the Birthday Cake Martini on page 136, use simple syrup, honey, melted chocolate, or even frosting. Any sticky liquid will work to make the seasoning adhere: pour the liquid into a shallow saucer, turn the glass upside down, and dip the rim into the liquid.

To add the seasoning, put the desired flavoring (salt, sugar, sprinkles, crushed candy, chili powder, lavender buds, etc.) in a clean, dry saucer with a larger circumference than that of the glass. Dip or roll the top edge of the moistened rim in the seasonings in the saucer and voilà: you've now added flavor and visual punch to your punch.

Glassware

Some of these drinks (like the Birthday Cake Martini) are suited for traditional glassware, like the martini glass. But be inspired by the doll you're celebrating and experiment with different glassware for drinks. This can go beyond classic cocktail glasses, like the highball, coupe, or flute. You can try ones you may already have, like mason jars, mugs, teacups, or a regular ol' cup. Get creative!

Conversation Starters

The original social gathering for early American women revolved around needlework, and the American Girl Historical Characters were there for it! Kirsten celebrates her birthday with friends in a quilting bee, Molly and her classmates find unity while knitting squares into a blanket for soldiers, and Josefina and her sisters heal their grief while sewing Mamá's colcha cloth.

In a sewing circle, needles move fast and lips move faster! Girls took the opportunity to chat about their personal lives, discuss what was going on around them, and share opinions about how America was changing and progressing. Conversation that grew out of sewing circles inspired women to get involved politically, using their needlework to support American troops during the Revolutionary War, the War of 1812, the Civil War, and World War I, and eventually helped give rise to the suffrage movement, with women using their skills to communicate demands for equality on sashes, banners, and handkerchiefs.

Today, gathering over a shared activity remains a ritual for women, whether that be catching up over community meetings, brunch, mani-pedis at the salon, volunteer work, facetime group hangouts, or—a hugely popular one—book clubs. Today, book lovers gather in person or in social media forums to discuss their favorite novels. That alone is remarkable when, up until 150 years ago, families may not have felt it was necessary to teach their daughters to read (let's give a *¡hurra!* to Tía Dolores for her literacy intervention on behalf of Josefina and her sisters). And, just like the sewing circle of the past, the talk in book clubs goes beyond the page, with members using the time for social connection, sharing the latest about their lives, trading opinions on pop culture, and discussing world events, all the while bonding over some munchies and sweet treats.

Whether you and your girls are crafting or discussing the latest American Girl book, these drinks and dishes are conversation starters.

Beautiful Braided Cinnamon Buns

KIRSTEN LARSON,
Historical Character 1854

MAKES 12 CINNAMON BUNS/ SWEETS AND DESSERTS

Cinnamon buns are an American Girl tradition! The sugary, buttery breakfast treats appear in many of the Historical Characters and the Girls of the Year books. At the American Girl Café, they serve mini cinnamon buns to you and your doll minutes after you are seated at the table. (Dessert for appetizers? A girl can dream—and make it a reality at the café!) And who better to pair this treat and introduce this cookbook than Kirsten Larson, an original Historical Character.

As the eldest daughter, Kirsten had the honor of surprising her family with a tray of sweet buns on St. Lucia's day, a Scandinavian holiday celebrated on December 13 each year. Early that morning, while it was still dark, Kirsten dressed as St. Lucia, complete with a white gown, a red sash, and a glowing candlelit wreath on her head to celebrate light and hope during the dark days of winter. Inspired by Kirsten's St. Lucia story, these cinnamon buns are a welcome and comforting treat to warm hearts, gather around, and share with friends.

INGREDIENTS

Dough

1 cup milk

¾ cup unsalted butter, softened

2 large eggs

4 cups bread flour

1 tablespoon instant dry yeast

¼ cup granulated sugar

1 teaspoon salt

Filling

½ cup unsalted butter, softened

1 cup brown sugar, packed

½ teaspoon vanilla extract

2 teaspoons ground cinnamon

Egg wash

1 egg

Topping

2 tablespoons powdered sugar, for dusting

RECIPE STEPS

1. Using a stand mixer with a dough hook, combine milk, butter, eggs, flour, yeast, granulated sugar, and salt. Mix on slowest speed for 2 minutes, then increase to medium speed and mix for another 4 to 6 minutes until the dough begins to come away from the side of the bowl. If sticky, add additional flour.

2. Form the dough into a ball and place into a large, greased bowl. Cover with a kitchen towel and let rise until it is twice the original size, approximately 45 minutes to an hour.

3. To make the filling, beat butter, brown sugar, vanilla extract, and cinnamon in a medium bowl. Set aside.

4. On a floured surface, roll the rested dough into a large horizontal rectangle, roughly 16 inches across and 12 inches top to bottom.

5. Spread the filling across the entire top of the dough.

6. Fold the dough over so that it will be stacked into three layers: Start by folding the bottom third of the dough rectangle over so that it rests just past the middle. If you have extra cinnamon filling, spread it on top of the newly exposed dough. Next, fold the top third of the dough over to what is now the bottom of the rectangle, completely enclosing the filling. The original dough rectangle should now be a long, tri-layered dough strip.

7. Using a rolling pin, slightly flatten the now three-layer dough.

8. Cut the dough vertically into 12 strips, each roughly 1½ inches across.

9. Next, without cutting all the way through one end, cut twice down the length of each 1½-inch strip to make three long strands on one end, with the other end uncut.

10. Braid the three strands together and, starting from the uncut side, roll up the dough into a bun.

11. Place each bun on a greased 17 x 12-inch baking sheet, leaving the braided side on top. Repeat to make 12 buns.

12. Cover the buns with a kitchen towel and let rise for 1 hour or until they double in size. When done rising, preheat oven to 350°F.

13. Beat egg in a small bowl. Brush each bun with the egg wash.

14. Bake for 20 to 25 minutes until golden-brown.

15. Place the cinnamon buns on a cooling rack for at least 5 minutes.

16. When cool, dust with powdered sugar.

17. Admire your handiwork and wish it were this easy to rebraid Kirsten's hair!

18. Devour your dolled-up treat.

KIRSTEN LARSON

The Kirsten Larson character was one of the three OGs (Original Girls, that is) introduced in 1986, when American Girl was still the Pleasant Company, along with Molly McIntire and Samantha Parkington. Her two looped braids are instantly recognizable and are a callback to her Swedish heritage. The prairie look was in style for most of the '80s, so Kirsten's light-blue prairie dress was historical and high fashion. If you were a Kirsten girl, you probably still feel the pangs of instant regret from taking out her braids (and the subsequent panic while trying to recreate the look), and you remember Kirsten's epic story and outfits—especially her St. Lucia gown and crown of candles.

Get Your Goat Cheese Dip

JOSEFINA MONTOYA,
Historical Character 1824

MAKES 6 SERVINGS/ APPETIZERS AND SNACKS

When it comes to aunting, Tía Dolores is the greatest of all time, but she's not the only "goat" in Josefina's life. When Tía Dolores first comes to visit, Josefina's archenemy Florecita—the "biggest, oldest, meanest goat" who is a "sneaky, nasty bully"—eats the flower arrangement Josefina made to welcome her. She confronts Florecita a few times—the yellow-eyed, sharp-horned meany really gets under her skin. Although Florecita causes some mishaps, she and her kid goat Sombrita eventually teach Josefina to have courage and an open heart. Using New Mexico chiles, this goat cheese dip is a reminder that even something with a bit of a kick can be rewarding and is the perfect munchie for girl gatherings. Just place it out of reach of hungry pets on the roam.

INGREDIENTS

¼ cup vegetable oil

5 dried New Mexico chiles, stemmed, seeded, and finely chopped (about ¼ cup) (substitute with other dried chiles or, if necessary, a 4-ounce can of green chiles, drained)

2 cloves garlic, chopped

8 ounces goat cheese, room temperature

2 tablespoons milk

¼ teaspoon salt

⅛ teaspoon black pepper

⅛ teaspoon cayenne pepper

⅛ teaspoon cumin

2 tablespoons toasted pine nuts, a few nuts reserved for garnish

½ teaspoon orange zest, for garnish

Sliced vegetables, chips, or bread toasts, for serving

RECIPE STEPS

1. Heat vegetable oil in a medium frying pan over medium heat. Once hot, add chiles for 2 minutes. Turn down heat to medium low and add garlic. After 30 seconds, remove from heat and let steep for 10 minutes.

2. Combine goat cheese, milk, salt, black pepper, cayenne pepper, cumin, and most of the pine nuts in a food processor. Spoon out chile and garlic pieces from the oil and add to the food processor, along with half the oil.

3. Blend on high until airy and smooth.

4. Transfer to a bowl and garnish with remaining oil, pine nuts, and orange zest.

5. Serve with vegetables, chips, or bread toasts.

JOSEFINA MONTOYA

In 1997, girls flipping through the American Girl catalog were drawn to a gorgeous new character: Josefina Montoya. As a citizen of Mexico in 1824, Josefina was American Girl's first Hispanic character, and her story takes place on her papá's rancho near Santa Fe. This area was a part of Mexico at that time until it was annexed by the United States in 1848 and became a US state in 1912. One of the first six characters introduced in the early years of the Pleasant Company, Josefina's look included mahogany hair braided to perfection with flowers or ribbons, gold hoop earrings that perfectly matched her necklace, and a colorful rebozo and sash. If your doll of choice was Josefina, you appreciate her sweet disposition and unique backstory.

Josefina's story is filled with hardships but also hope. A year after the death of Mamá, she and her family are grieving deeply—that is until Tía Dolores comes to visit. Mamá's sister steps in as the mother figure they all miss and crave, and she teaches Josefina and her sisters to garden, bake, embroider, sew, read, and, most of all, welcome second chances.

Salmon Spears

KAYA'ATON'MY,
Historical Character 1764

MAKES 4 SERVINGS/ MAIN MUNCHIES

In Kaya's time, the Nimíipuu made an annual trek to Celilo Falls, where salmon splash and spawn and Indigenous tribes gathered to fish, feast, trade, and celebrate together. Salmon swim through Kaya's story. Everyone worked together to secure fish for the winter. The men speared the salmon. The women gutted and prepared the salmon for roasting, then dried the salmon to store for the winter.

The stories of summers in Celilo Falls serve as a reminder of the salmon's vital importance to the Nimíipuu, which carries into their culture today.

INGREDIENTS

1½ to 2 pounds skinless salmon fillet, 12 inches long

1 tablespoon sesame oil

2 tablespoons soy sauce

1 tablespoon maple syrup

2 teaspoons chili garlic sauce

1 tablespoon extra-virgin olive oil

1 teaspoon sesame seeds, for garnish

2 green onions, sliced, for garnish

RECIPE STEPS

1. Rinse and dry salmon.

2. With the fillets resting horizontally left to right on a cutting board, slice them vertically into 8 equal strips, each about 1½ inches wide.

3. Place a skewer into the bottom of each salmon "finger" and push it up until it reaches the top without breaking through the far end.

4. In a wide shallow bowl, mix sesame oil, soy sauce, maple syrup, and chili garlic sauce. Place salmon fingers into the mixture. Cover with plastic wrap and marinate between 30 minutes and 6 hours.

5. When done marinating, heat olive oil in a large nonstick skillet over medium heat.

6. Place each salmon finger into the skillet, cooking each side 1 minute before rotating. Repeat on all four sides of each salmon finger.

7. Pour any remaining marinade into the skillet for 1 minute and toss to coat salmon in the marinade.

8. Garnish with sesame seeds and sliced green onions then serve.

KAYA

Released in 2002, Kaya'aton'my (Kaya) is American Girl's eighth Historical Character, but because her story takes place in 1764, this makes her the "first" American Girl. Her shiny long black braids tied with abalone shells, her colorful necklace with beads made to look like porcupine quills, and her buckskin-colored dress trimmed with fringe show that Kaya and her people live in tune with nature. Kaya girls are an adventurous bunch, inspired by her daring horseback race, skill in tracking her little brothers when they are lost, and heart-stopping rescue of Speaking Rain from a raging river.

American Girl asked the Nimíipuu for permission and help in telling Kaya's story. A group of tribal elders, educators, and historians reviewed Kaya's stories as well as every detail of her collection, from hair ties to moccasins.

Fresh Start Lemon-Limeade

CHRISSA MAXWELL,
Girl of the Year 2009

MAKES 4 DRINKS/ COCKTAILS AND MOCKTAILS

When new-kid-on-the-block Chrissa experiences bullying at her school in Minnesota, she uses her artistic streak to find a way to stand up against it. With new friends Gwen and Sonali, they gather to make headbands to wear to school and demonstrate the strength of their friendship in the face of bullying and represent a call for kindness. Chrissa finds that when you take a stand and challenge the status quo for what is right, true friends will follow.

Inspired by Chrissa's new home state Minnesota's signature cocktail, the Minnesota Bootleg, a bright, tart lemon-lime beverage developed during Prohibition, this refreshing beverage is ideal for conversations about meaningful change with friends.

This recipe makes four drinks. For a single serving, the ratio is 2 ounces of the lemonade mix, 2 ounces of alcohol, and 2 ounces of club soda.

INGREDIENTS

½ cup lemon juice, freshly squeezed (about 3 lemons)

¼ cup lime juice, freshly squeezed (about 2 limes)

¼ to ⅓ cup agave nectar

⅛ cup (2 tablespoons) fresh, washed mint leaves, compacted to make full

1 cup vodka, gin, or bourbon, for cocktail

1 cup club soda

RECIPE STEPS

1. Combine lemon juice, lime juice, agave nectar, and mint leaves in a blender. For the cocktail, add ¼ cup agave; for the mocktail, add ⅓ cup agave. Blend until mint leaves are chopped into tiny bits.

2. For the cocktail, add alcohol of choice, and blend again.

3. Divide into four rocks glasses filled with ice. Top with club soda.

CHRISSA MAXWELL

Chrissa Maxwell enrolls in a new school in Minnesota on Valentine's Day, but she gets no love from the Queen Bees of the fourth grade. Chrissa renames the group the Mean Bees after they steal her Valentine cards and insult classmate Gwen. As the girls ramp up their efforts to bully Chrissa, she finds comfort with her nana's llamas: Checkers, Cosmos, and baby cria, Starburst.

Chrissa uses the llama wool for her knitting and sewing projects (her collection includes a sewing machine and craft center), perfect for making hats to go with her snowsuit for snow-tubing days. All these sporty distractions make for great accessories, but something else comes with being an athlete—the courage to face an opponent. When Chrissa stands up to the bullies by initiating a kindness campaign that the whole school supports, the Queen Bees join in, finally learning how to be Minnesota nice.

Harlem Cocktail

CLAUDIE WELLS,
Historical Character 1922

MAKES 2 DRINKS/ COCKTAILS AND MOCKTAILS

Living in Harlem in the 1920s, Claudie is witnessing an era of Black creative expression that inspires today. In the late nineteenth and early twentieth centuries, millions of Black Americans migrated north, and they built communities where they worked as artists, business owners, and professionals. Harlem, in upper Manhattan, had a unique pull, attracting and encouraging Black artists and talent to thrive.

The Harlem Cocktail is inspired by a Prohibition-era drink served at Harlem's famed Cotton Club. The drink evolved into the pineapple-heavy Harlem No. 2 and No. 3, but the original is much jazzier. Make a few to share with friends during a get-together.

INGREDIENTS

3 ounces whiskey
3 ounces gin
1 ounce lime juice
1 ounce simple syrup
1 egg white

RECIPE STEPS

1. Into a cocktail shaker, pour whiskey, gin, lime juice, simple syrup, and egg white.
2. Dry shake (no ice) vigorously for 30 seconds.
3. Add ice and shake to cool, but gently to retain foam.
4. Strain into two chilled cocktail glasses.

CLAUDIE WELLS

Harlem's got talent! But does Claudie Wells? While this nine-year-old is insecure about her artistic cred, American Girl fans know this girl is going places! The eighteenth Historical Character is living during the Harlem Renaissance, the era in which Black creatives flocked to Harlem to live a life of free self-expression. She loves reading and writing and activities that allow her imagination to soar.

Blaireberry Muffins

BLAIRE WILSON,
Girl of the Year 2019

MAKES 12 MUFFINS/ SWEETS AND DESSERTS

When it comes to food, Blaire has flair. Known for farm-fancy dishes, she cohosts cooking segments with her mom on the Pleasant View YouTube cooking channel where viewers have taken to renaming blueberries "blaireberries." In honor of Blaire, this comfort food recipe is farm to table, and the lemon glaze adds a touch of fancy, perfect for breakfast after a sleepover or afternoon tea with friends.

INGREDIENTS

Muffins

2 cups flour

1 tablespoon baking powder

1 teaspoon lemon zest

¾ cup sugar

½ teaspoon salt

½ cup unsalted butter, softened

1 cup milk

2 eggs

1 teaspoon vanilla extract

1½ cups blueberries

Glaze

1 cup powdered sugar

⅛ cup lemon juice, freshly squeezed (about ½ lemon)

RECIPE STEPS

1. Preheat oven to 400°F.
2. Mix flour, baking powder, lemon zest, sugar, and salt in a bowl. Set aside.
3. Using an electric mixer, beat butter and milk in a separate bowl.
4. Add in eggs and vanilla extract; continue mixing.
5. Stir the liquid into the flour mixture, blending the two.
6. Fold in blueberries.
7. Spoon the batter into a 12-cup muffin pan.
8. Bake for 15 to 20 minutes.
9. While baking, make the glaze: in a fresh bowl, mix powdered sugar with lemon juice.
10. After muffins cool for 5 to 10 minutes, brush glaze over muffins.

BLAIRE WILSON

Blaire Wilson is the American Girl of the Year most likely to pull together a dazzling celebration or cozy girls night. At ten years old, the red-headed character is full of ideas on how to make memorable moments extra special, using the fresh fruits and vegetables grown on her family farm to make delicious, healthy dishes for the guests of the family-run Pleasant View Farm Bed and Breakfast in Upstate New York. But when two of the farm's employees, down-to-earth Cat and upper-crust Gabe, decide to get married, Blaire "idea sparks" a wedding theme to blend their worlds together: "farm fancy"!

Blaire's country cute playsets are a cook's dream: a fully stocked chef's kitchen, restaurant, garden, and wedding reception hall, complete with a three-tiered wedding cake.

CHAPTER 2

Take-a-Break Bevvies and Bites

Sometimes, all you wanted to do was take your doll with you to school to keep you company. You couldn't wait to rush back home to be with your dolls, dreaming about what outfit you'd change them into that day. Or maybe during your lunch or recess break, you took out one of the books and delved into one of the worlds of American Girl. Although you are no longer a grade-school student, there are still things that require your attention, concentration, and brainstorming. Whether planning a pitch, setting a grad-school study session, or organizing a networking night, these character-inspired recipes offer the right balance of fun and focus to keep you motivated or offer you a yummy break.

Addy's AlphaBites

ADDY WALKER,
Historical Character 1864

**MAKES 6 SERVINGS/
APPETIZERS AND SNACKS**

When Addy arrived in Philadelphia, she longed to learn to read. Falling in love with words and reading, she becomes a champion speller, winning her fourth-grade spelling bee. Academic success doesn't happen overnight. It takes dedication and a creatively delicious approach. Addy created cookies in the shape of the letters of the alphabet—allowing her to learn while spending time with Momma. Like Addy, eat the alphabet to help you study, brainstorm, or prep for a presentation.

INGREDIENTS

1 ¼ cups Greek yogurt
¼ cup honey
1 teaspoon vanilla extract
⅛ teaspoon ground cinnamon
⅛ teaspoon sugar

Fruits of the alphabet
(pick your favorites*):
Apples or apricots
Bananas, blackberries, or blueberries
Cherries
(D is for dip, E is for easy, F is for fruit!)
Grapes
Kiwi
Mango
Pineapple
Strawberries

RECIPE STEPS

1. In a small mixing bowl, mix yogurt, honey, vanilla extract, cinnamon, and sugar together until smooth.

2. Refrigerate for 30 minutes.

3. Serve with fruit.

*Note that melons and citrus fruits don't pair as well with this dip.

ADDY WALKER

Wearing a cinnamon-pink dress and lace pantalettes as sweet as her kind expression, Addy Walker made a splash as American Girl's first Black character. Her fabulous hair was gorgeously braided into a low back bun, which would stay intact when she completed her look with a straw bonnet or hat. While her assortment of dresses, cowrie necklace, and golden earrings were fun to play with, the truth is, they were only part of Addy's story. Through Connie Porter's riveting story of Addy's escape from slavery and her unshakable belief in love and family, we understood what courage and confidence truly meant.

Figgy Piggy Treats

NICKI FLEMING,
Girl of the Year 2007

**MAKES 8 SERVINGS/
APPETIZERS AND SNACKS**

Ten-year-old Nicki helps her mother train a puppy to become a service animal, a task she hasn't handled before. Although there are ups and downs, training Sprocket brings her incredible happiness and incredible heartbreak, as he completes his training and leaves to become an assistance dog to a girl who uses a wheelchair. Inspired by the treats she rewards Sprocket with during training that "look sort of like a pig wrapped in a blanket," and elevated with fig and goat cheese, these scrumptious snacks will be crowd-pleasers after a hard day's work.

INGREDIENTS

1 8-ounce tube crescent rolls

4 slices thick-cut bacon

1¼ cups red wine

2 tablespoons honey, divided

1 pint dried figs

5 ounces honey goat cheese

2 tablespoons half-and-half

1 jalapeño pepper, minced

2 tablespoons fresh rosemary needles, chopped

½ teaspoon black pepper

1 large egg

NICKI FLEMING

Is it a coincidence that the same year teenage Taylor Swift broke into the collective consciousness through country music, American Girl gave us a Girl of the Year with similarly shaded dark-blonde hair with curling-iron curls who lived in a home on the range? Dressed in cowgirl cool (pink suede chaps! purple boots!) and equipped with a can-do attitude, rancher Nicki Fleming made being given too much responsibility look easy—to her detriment. Her heavy chore load includes brushing the horses, cleaning the pigsty, doing the dishes, cooking dinner, and helping her brother Adam with his math homework every night—a lot of work for her. But also, a lot of suggested play for us!

RECIPE STEPS

1. Preheat oven to 350°F.
2. Unroll crescent roll dough on a floured surface and roll out to ⅛-inch thickness with a rolling pin.
3. Cut dough into 8 equal-sized squares.
4. Use nonstick cooking spray to grease a muffin pan. Lay each dough square into the muffin pan so the edges rise up to form a cup.
5. Bake for 8 minutes.
6. At the same time, arrange bacon strips on a pan lined with foil. Bake until crisp, about 12 minutes. Let bacon cool and chop.
7. Remove the muffin pan from oven and use a small spoon to reshape the dough to create a cup to fill with ingredients. Keep oven on.
8. In a medium saucepan, stir wine and 1 tablespoon honey over medium heat until boiling.
9. Reduce heat to simmer; add figs to the saucepan and simmer for 15 minutes. Remove figs from the saucepan and cut into thin slices.
10. In a small bowl, beat together the goat cheese, half-and-half, and jalapeño until smooth.
11. Dollop a spoonful of the goat cheese mixture into each dough-lined cup.
12. Sprinkle a few dried fig slices and a few pieces of bacon on each cup.
13. Top each cup with a sprinkle of rosemary and ground pepper.
14. Beat egg in a bowl and brush the exposed dough edges of each cup with egg wash.
15. Bake for 3 minutes. Let cool.
16. Plate the cups, and drizzle each cup with remaining honey before serving.

Brain Power Garden Pizza

LANIE HOLLAND,
Girl of the Year 2010

MAKES 6 SERVINGS/ MAIN MUNCHIES

Lanie Holland's life dream is to become a wildlife researcher—which leads to a love of everything that is outdoors, including the animals and plant life found near her home, down to the lowliest milkweed and ladybug. When younger sister Emily refuses to eat anything that isn't pizza, Lanie realizes that a creative solution lies right in the backyard. With the help of Aunt Hannah, they plant a vegetable garden to grow their own tasty and healthy pizza toppings. Try this delicious interpretation, and like Lanie, observe which toppings you and your friends like best. Packed with brain-boosting and healthy ingredients, this yummy recipe will get you through the most difficult of tasks.

INGREDIENTS

Dough

½ cup warm water

1 teaspoon active dry yeast

1 teaspoon honey

¼ cup extra-virgin olive oil

1¾ cups flour

A pinch of kosher salt

Romesco sauce

12 ounces jarred, roasted red peppers, drained

14 ounces canned fire-roasted tomatoes, drained

1 cup raw almonds

¼ cup flat leaf parsley, coarsely chopped

1 teaspoon red pepper flakes

2 garlic cloves, chopped

Juice of ½ lemon

1 teaspoon sherry vinegar

1 teaspoon kosher salt

½ teaspoon black pepper

1 teaspoon smoked paprika

¼ cup extra-virgin olive oil

Toppings

½ fresh red bell pepper, sliced

3 medium button mushrooms, sliced

¼ cup red onion, sliced

1 cup sliced cherry tomatoes

½ cup jarred artichoke hearts, sliced in half

¼ cup plus 1 tablespoon extra-virgin olive oil, divided

Salt and black pepper, to taste

½ cup chopped feta cheese, cut into ½-inch chunks

1 cup arugula

½ cup thinly sliced fresh basil

⅛ cup balsamic glaze

RECIPE STEPS

To make the dough:

1. The night before cooking and serving the pizza, in a large bowl combine warm water, yeast, honey, and olive oil. Mix until yeast dissolves, and let sit for 10 minutes.

2. Add flour and salt. Mix until the dough makes a ball.

3. Remove to a lightly floured surface and knead for 3 to 5 minutes.

4. Place in a lightly greased bowl, cover, and refrigerate overnight.

5. The next day, remove the dough from the refrigerator and use a rolling pin to shape the dough into one round pizza crust.

6. Spread the dough on a greased 16-inch pizza pan.

To make the romesco sauce:

1. Combine roasted red peppers, fire-roasted tomatoes, almonds, parsley, red pepper flakes, garlic, lemon juice, sherry vinegar, salt, black pepper, and paprika in a food processor.

2. Pulse until mostly blended, then process while gradually adding the olive oil until the romesco reaches a loose, paste-like consistency.

To make the pizza:

1. Preheat oven to 350°F.

2. Spread red bell pepper, mushrooms, red onion, cherry tomatoes, and artichoke hearts on a separate sheet pan, toss with ¼ cup olive oil, and season with salt and black pepper.

3. Brush the edges of the pizza dough with olive oil.

4. Bake both the pizza dough and the vegetables for 10 minutes.

5. Remove the pizza dough, now a lightly baked crust, from oven, and continue to bake the vegetables for 10 more minutes.

6. Spread the romesco sauce on the pizza crust. Store the remaining romesco sauce in an airtight container in the refrigerator for up to a week for use in another recipe.

7. Remove the vegetables from oven.

8. Increase oven temperature to 450°F.

9. Top the pizza with the roasted vegetables. Sprinkle feta cheese on top of the pizza.

10. Bake the pizza for 10 minutes, or until the crust is golden-brown.

11. Toss arugula and basil in a small bowl with 1 tablespoon olive oil and season with a pinch of salt and black pepper.

12. Once the crust is golden-brown, remove the pizza from oven. Top with the arugula-basil mix, drizzle with balsamic glaze, and serve.

LANIE HOLLAND

Girl of the Year 2010 Lanie Holland gave us more than dreams of walking a pet bunny on a leash around the neighborhood—with her "outside genes," she gave us a love of the outdoors. Achieving her career goal is off to a good start when she takes field notes on the metamorphosis of the caterpillars in little sister Emily's first-grade classroom terrarium. What starts as a mildly interesting project becomes a passion as Lanie becomes more intrigued by monarch butterflies, and she plants a garden with milkweed and wildflowers in her backyard with her aunt, an ornithologist. Any time observing and spending time in nature is time well spent for Lanie. By bringing Lanie onto the scene, American Girl encouraged us to get outside and reminded us of the wonders of exploring the great outdoors. And with Lanie's cute nature outfits and Aunt Hannah's awesomely detailed RV, we were all happy campers!

Crunch-Time Cucumber Salad

CORINNE TAN,
Girl of the Year 2022

MAKES 4 SERVINGS/
SIDES AND SALADS

Corinne Tan knows how to keep cool as a cucumber when it's crunch time. She stays calm through the rough moments—teaching her dog, Flurry, to be a rescue animal; remaining steady during her mom's divorce; moving to a new house; having her mom open a new restaurant; and, scariest of all, keeping her wits when she gets lost on a mountain. Corinne demonstrates that when it's time to focus on the problem at hand, staying cool is the way to go.

This recipe is likely to be on the menu at her mother's Chinese street food restaurant, Kuai Le—which means "happiness" and "soon." Every bite of this umami dish translates into a refreshing delight, ideal for moments when you need a reset.

INGREDIENTS

- 2 cloves garlic, minced
- 1 scallion, sliced on the bias
- 2 English cucumbers, peeled and sliced
- 2 tablespoons soy sauce
- 2 tablespoons garlic chili sauce
- 1 teaspoon salt
- 1 teaspoon sesame seeds
- 1½ tablespoons brown sugar, lightly packed
- 1 tablespoon Mirin
- 2 tablespoons white vinegar
- 1 teaspoon sesame oil

RECIPE STEPS

1. Combine ingredients in a medium bowl.
2. Chill for 30 minutes and serve.

CORINNE TAN

Corinne Tan is a Chinese American Girl of the Year from 2022 who is a fixture on the ski slopes of Aspen, a result of having a dad who is the most in-demand instructor at Buttermilk Ski Resort. Just as her dad is teaching her and little sister Gwynn how to ski switch (translation: backward!), her life does a 180. Her mom is remarrying and having a baby, and Corinne worries about the changes coming with a blended family, including bouncing back and forth between two homes.

Corinne keeps her worries to herself, but that bright blue streak in her hair represents a boldness that can't be contained. She learns to stand up to racism and misinformation, making her an example of courage and relatability for girls of today.

Tumble-Tini

McKENNA BROOKS,
Girl of the Year 2012

**MAKES 1 DRINK/
COCKTAILS AND MOCKTAILS**

McKenna lives in Seattle (cue the stylish doll-size raincoat and umbrella), which is famously home of the Space Needle (where she celebrates a gymnastics win with friends and family), the first Starbucks, and plenty of other artisanal and boutique coffee shops! And the love of coffee runs in the family—her mom owns a coffee shop. This delicious espresso martini is a nod to McKenna's hometown, her family, and her friends. Share this drink with your friends when you need that pick-me-up during a grind session.

INGREDIENTS

2 ounces vodka

1 ounce coffee liqueur

1½ ounces Irish cream

2 ounces espresso or coffee, freshly brewed (cold brew works, but sacrifices flavor and foam)

3 coffee beans, for garnish

RECIPE STEPS

1. Pour vodka, coffee liqueur, Irish cream, and espresso or coffee into a cocktail shaker. Dry shake (no ice) for 30 seconds to create froth.

2. Add ice to a shaker. Shake again, no more than 20 seconds.

3. Serve in a chilled martini glass, making sure that ample foam tops the drink. Add three coffee beans to keep you awake through midnight!

McKENNA BROOKS

McKenna Brooks flips for gymnastics, on track to join the Shooting Stars Gym competitive team. However, at school, her homework is doing cartwheels around her. Embarrassed that she needs help, she keeps her tutoring sessions a secret from besties Toulane and Sierra. McKenna is walking a balance beam between gymnastics, school, and friends—and she finally falls, figuratively and literally, breaking an ankle.

McKenna is stuck in a metaphorical backbend: life is upside down. But tutor Josie teaches McKenna to apply the visualization skills she uses in gymnastics to reading, and her grades improve. Josie, a wheelchair user who also rides horses, educates McKenna that hard work and self-belief can help her overcome her challenges. When her cast comes off, McKenna sticks the landing at her gymnastics competition. McKenna's doll accessories—like her cute pink crutches, a foot cast, and a wheelchair—paved a way for acceptance of disabled play. Fun fact: we later learn that McKenna attends college in Minnesota, where she becomes the gymnastics coach for 2024 Girl of the Year Lila Monetti!

Red Rover Fuel

LUCIANA VEGA,
Girl of the Year 2018

MAKES 1 DRINK/
COCKTAILS AND MOCKTAILS

With a purple streak illuminating her raven hair like a comet lighting up the sky, eleven-year-old rocket scientist Luciana Vega proved to be out of this world. Her goal is to be the first girl on Mars, and when she's named captain of the all-girl Red Rover team at her space camp, it's one giant step closer for girlkind! Revel in the red planet and stay alert with this Mars-colored energy drink. Tart cherry juice is known to improve heart health and provide faster muscle recovery. And with green tea as a base, this drink keeps stamina up and enhances focus to prevent spacing out.

INGREDIENTS

¼ cup tart cherry juice*

¼ cup cranberry juice*

2 tablespoons lime juice, freshly squeezed

½ cup green tea

1 tablespoon simple syrup*

½ cup sparkling water

Mint leaves, for garnish

Lime slice, for garnish

RECIPE STEPS

1. In a tall glass, stir tart cherry juice, cranberry juice, lime juice, green tea, simple syrup, and ice.

2. Top with sparkling water.

3. Sprinkle mint leaves on top. Garnish with a lime slice. Sip and power up!

*If like Luciana and the robot-building challenge, you're on a tight deadline, save time by substituting ½ cup premade cranberry-cherry juice, such as Ocean Spray. If the cranberry-cherry juice or green tea is sweetened, eliminate the simple syrup.

LUCIANA VEGA

The STEMsational Girl of the Year's popularity was so high, she had the unprecedented record of not being retired for nearly four years. The future astronaut attends not one but *two* space camps. Space camp isn't just a zero-gravity flight delight; it's building robots, growing hydroponic plants, and mastering SCUBA for survival. As the captain of the all-girl Red Rover team, Luciana Vega learns a lot about leadership when she jumps to conclusions about a rival team's intentions—unintentionally sabotaging their chances. The Red Rovers rally, helping the team they'd accidentally put at a disadvantage win the competition. Just as in science, lessons come from failure, and Luciana learns that astronauts must always find a way to work together, even if they don't get along.

Sweet and Spicy Coconut Coffee

COCONUT,
the American Girl mascot

**MAKES 1 DRINK/
COCKTAILS AND MOCKTAILS**

The adorable white dog Coconut is a favorite play pet for die-hard American Girl fans. What is guaranteed to lift your spirits and energy through a workday? A playful puppy and a hot mug of coffee! American Girl constant companion Coconut (or Coconut Chip, depending on your year) fetches some cozy in a cup with this recipe that's sweet, white, and frothy like the pup that pairs with every doll—but go slow with the hot honey, it's got a bite!

INGREDIENTS

2 ounces coconut creamer

¼ ounce hot honey, as in spicy, not heated

8 ounces coffee, freshly brewed

RECIPE STEPS

1. If you have access to a frother, pour coconut creamer into a mixing glass and froth for 60 seconds.

2. Add hot honey. For those who like their coffee to bark without so much bite, substitute regular honey.

3. Pour the frothy mixture into a mug of hot coffee. Lightly stir. Start sipping!

K9
Krunchies
DOG SNACKS

CHAPTER 3

Girls Got Game

Whether it was an entire gymnastics center or a sensational Team USA soccer outfit, American Girl offered many options to make dolls sporty. Having your doll match your game outfit made competitions or practices that much sweeter. Not only that, but American Girls themselves are gamer girls and girls who've got game! Whether you're smashing quarters like Courtney, shooting hoops like Julie, surfing like Joss, or tailgating before the big game, these treats have spirit, yes they do—and now, so do you.

Pac-Manicotti

COURTNEY MOORE,
Historical Character 1986

**MAKES 10 SERVINGS/
MAIN MUNCHIES**

One of the greatest entertainment products for kids of the 1980s was, without a doubt, Pac-Man. The classic arcade game featuring a giant yellow dot living in a gobble-or-be-gobbled world stands the test of time, and it's the favorite pastime of Historical Character Courtney Moore. Inspired by mall culture and Courtney's favorite game, this stuffed manicotti (a little more elaborate than the offerings at mall-favorite Sbarro) will have friends gobbling up this avatar-inspired pasta like they're dots—and munching on a meatball as a protein-filled power pellet. Sprinkle parsley across the top; unlike Courtney's same-named guinea pig, the herb is a pleasant-scented enhancement.

INGREDIENTS

½ pound ground beef
½ cup breadcrumbs
½ teaspoon garlic powder
½ teaspoon onion powder
½ teaspoon dried basil
½ teaspoon dried oregano
½ teaspoon dried parsley
1 teaspoon red pepper flakes, divided
2 cloves garlic, minced, divided
1 large egg
2 teaspoons salt, divided
2 teaspoons black pepper, divided
2 tablespoons extra-virgin olive oil
10 ounces frozen chopped spinach, thawed
15 ounces ricotta cheese
1½ cups mozzarella cheese, shredded, divided
1 cup Parmesan cheese, shredded
10 manicotti shells
1 24-ounce jar marinara sauce
1½ cups water
1 tablespoon fresh parsley, chopped

RECIPE STEPS

1. Preheat oven to 350°F.

2. In a large bowl, mix ground beef, breadcrumbs, garlic powder, onion powder, basil, oregano, parsley, ½ teaspoon red pepper flakes, half the garlic, egg, and 1 teaspoon each of salt and black pepper.

3. Divide the hamburger mixture into four equal portions, rolling each into a meatball.

4. Heat olive oil in a large skillet over medium heat. When hot, add the four meatballs, browning each side before turning, until all sides are browned. Remove from heat and set aside.

5. Tightly squeeze spinach over a mesh strainer to remove all excess water. Dry with paper towels.

6. In another large bowl, combine remaining red pepper flakes, remaining garlic, remaining salt and black pepper, spinach, ricotta, ½ cup mozzarella, and Parmesan.

7. Using a spoon or piping bag (or fill a plastic sandwich bag and cut off one bottom corner), fill each of the uncooked manicotti shells with the cheese mixture.

8. In a 13 x 9-inch baking dish, oriented horizontally left to right, start on the left side and place the first manicotti at a 45-degree angle such that the bottom of the manicotti shell touches the middle left edge of the baking dish and the top of the shell rests flush against the top of the baking dish, a few inches to the right of the top left of the dish. Place a second manicotti shell at a 45-degree angle beneath the first shell, such that the top of the manicotti shell touches the middle-left edge of the dish, and the bottom of the shell lay flush against the bottom of the pan. Place the remaining shells parallel to the first two, four on the top, four on the bottom, leaving the "mouth" of the "Pac-Man" open to the right.

9. Place the four meatballs in a row on the right side of the pan, ready to be "eaten" by the Pac-Manicottis. The ingredients in the pan should look something like this:

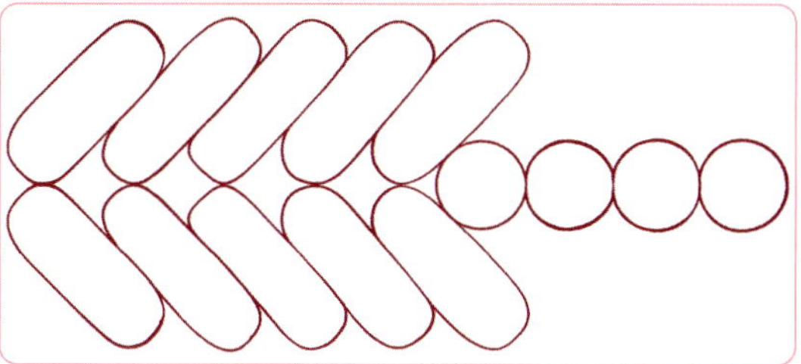

10. Cover the shells and meatballs with the marinara sauce. Add 1½ cups water. Cover with aluminum foil. Bake for 1 hour.

11. Remove from oven and remove aluminum foil. Spoon watery sauce at the bottom of dish on top of the shells and meatballs. Sprinkle 1 cup mozzarella on top of shells and meatballs, then return, uncovered, to oven for 20 minutes.

12. Remove from oven, let cool for 5 minutes, sprinkle with fresh parsley, and serve.

PAC-MAN
LIP SMACKER
Maureen
FOR
MAYOR
STEREO

COURTNEY MOORE

Courtney Moore is a spunky girl growing up in the '80s, and if her neon tights and scrunchie-adorned ponytail don't give that away, her love for the coin-operated games at the mall surely do. In the '80s, a giant indoor shopping center was *the* hang, no matter what state you lived in. Kids' domain was the arcade, where they'd compete for the high score in Centipede, Space Invaders, Donkey Kong, and Courtney's favorite, Pac-Man. Courtney loves them all, but she just can't understand why there aren't more girl characters in the games. Inspired by the superheroes that light up her game screens, Courtney creates her own heroine: space explorer Crystal Starshooter, in honor of Christa McAuliffe. Crystal travels the galaxy to discover and gather rare items to save planet Earth. By creating Crystal's adventures, Courtney learns how to stand up to the challenges in her own world, including her dad moving farther away for a better job, sharing a room with her moody stepsister, and helping her mom run for mayor.

Slam Dunk Spinach Salad

JULIE ALBRIGHT,
Historical Character 1974

**MAKES 4 SERVINGS/
SIDES AND SALADS**

Julie is a Historical Character who fights for her right to play on the school's basketball team—even though the coach says it's for boys only. What causes mean the most to you? Fuel up before you stand up and speak out with this power-packed salad, inspired by Julie's winning skills, on and off the court. Whether you're raising your voice to cheer for your team or a cause or need a delicious and healthy meal before jumping into practice or a game, this nutritious, delicious salad is a slam dunk.

INGREDIENTS

1 cup raspberries, divided
½ cup extra-virgin olive oil
¼ cup sherry vinegar
1 shallot, thinly sliced, divided
½ teaspoon salt, divided
½ teaspoon black pepper, divided
6 cups fresh baby spinach
1 cup strawberries, halved
½ cup blueberries
⅓ cup crumbled goat cheese
¼ cup roughly chopped walnuts or pecans

RECIPE STEPS

1. To prepare the vinaigrette, add ½ cup raspberries, olive oil, sherry vinegar, ½ shallot, ¼ teaspoon salt, and ¼ teaspoon black pepper to a food processor. Blend until it reaches the consistency of a salad dressing.

2. Add spinach, remaining raspberries, strawberries, blueberries, remaining shallot, goat cheese, and walnuts or pecans to a large mixing bowl. Season with remaining salt and black pepper and toss.

3. Toss the salad with the vinaigrette. Serve.

JULIE ALBRIGHT

Julie Albright is a "hoopster" with baller moves. Her new elementary school doesn't have a girls basketball team, and she must persuade appropriately named Coach Manley that the new law, Title IX, means he has to allow her to play with the boys. She starts a petition, and 150 signatures and a lot of bravery later, Julie wins—and an activist is born. She follows this up by raising awareness and money to save a family of bald eagles and runs for school president with her friend Joy. Dressed in groovy threads, like a peace sign tank, crocheted vest, and bell-bottoms, Julie stylishly reminds girls to fight for their rights and be the change they want to see.

H-E-Double Hockey Sticks-A Hot Buffalo Wings

MIA ST. CLAIR,
Girl of the Year 2008

MAKES 6–8 SERVINGS/ APPETIZERS AND SNACKS

Mia St. Clair is sweet and humble—only her red hair signals her fire inside! Growing up in a hockey-loving family who live to put the biscuit in the basket, this lightly freckled powerhouse has the sauce to rule the rink. Her kindness makes her the favorite coach giving skating lessons to little kids, but Mia wants more. She makes a bold choice—to pass on the pads and, instead, axel with elegance. Serving these juicy, sizzling, and spicy wings is a hat trick for the hungry. No doubt, Mia and her older brothers would gobble down these wings faster than a puck sliding past a distracted goalie. This dish calls for chicken but can easily be made vegetarian by substituting cauliflower.

INGREDIENTS

2 tablespoons unsalted butter
1 clove garlic, minced
1 teaspoon salt, divided
1 teaspoon black pepper, divided
¼ cup hot sauce
½ teaspoon cayenne powder
¼ teaspoon cumin
1 tablespoon Worcestershire sauce
¼ teaspoon corn starch
¼ cup extra-virgin olive oil
24 chicken wings (drums and flats)

RECIPE STEPS

1. Melt butter in a small pan over medium-low heat. Once melted, add garlic and a pinch of salt and black pepper. Cook for 2 minutes, stirring often.

2. Pour the garlic-butter mixture into a large mixing bowl. Add hot sauce, cayenne powder, cumin, Worcestershire sauce, corn starch, and remaining salt and black pepper. Whisk together well. Set aside.

3. Heat olive oil in a large skillet over medium-high heat. Once up to temperature, add half the wings. Brown on each side for 2 minutes, then set aside. Add the rest of the wings to the skillet and repeat.

4. Once the wings are browned, reduce heat to medium, and add all the wings back into the pan. Cover and cook 10 to 12 minutes, turning three times.

5. Once cooked through, add wings to the mixing bowl with the hot sauce. Toss to coat and serve hot.

MIA ST. CLAIR

As the youngest child and only daughter, Mia St. Clair decides to carve her own path. There's a full support system (and AG hockey outfit!) if she wanted to follow in her family's footsteps and rise through the ranks to become a hockey champ. But she's more interested in succeeding at a sport outside of her family's genetic code. She sticks to the ice—she is a "rink rat" living in Upstate New York, after all—and tries to find her footing as a figure skater (giving us a sparkly skater dress and a hairstyling kit for hours of happiness shaping buns, braids, and curl creations). What she lacks in confidence, she makes up for in gumption and grit. Enduring teasing from her brothers and bullying from a rival, she reminds us that we should follow our happiness, not follow what others want us to do.

Surf and Defend Your Turf Nachos

KAILEY HOPKINS,
Girl of the Year 2003

MAKES 6 SERVINGS/ APPETIZERS AND SNACKS

Boogie-boarding enthusiast Kailey and her dad love eating shrimp, which she learns are a valuable part of the food chain. She's enthusiastic about protecting the tide pools and the creatures who live in them, each one important to maintaining the ecosystem. This SoCal twist on a classic is a tasty balance of all the food groups. A recipe that makes the argument that nachos are healthy? Fantabulous!

INGREDIENTS

¼ cup lime juice

3 tablespoons vegetable oil, divided

1 tablespoon white vinegar

1 tablespoon soy sauce

½ teaspoon cayenne powder

½ teaspoon cumin

1 teaspoon salt, divided

1 teaspoon black pepper, divided

1 pound skirt or flank steak

16 shrimp, peeled and deveined

1 tablespoon Cajun seasoning

1 15-ounce bag tortilla chips, divided

1½ cups Cheddar cheese, shredded, divided

1 cup Monterey Jack cheese, shredded, divided

2 medium tomatoes, diced, divided

2 jalapeño peppers, sliced, divided

½ cup red onion, chopped, divided

3 green onions, chopped, for garnish

1 avocado, diced, for garnish

RECIPE STEPS

To make the steak:

1. To prepare the marinade, mix lime juice, 2 tablespoons vegetable oil, white vinegar, soy sauce, cayenne powder, cumin, and half the salt and black pepper in a small bowl.

2. Place steak in a baking dish and add the marinade. Mix well, cover with plastic wrap, and refrigerate for 1 to 2 hours.

3. Heat ½ tablespoon vegetable oil in a large deep skillet over medium-high heat. Once hot, cook steak for 3 to 4 minutes on each side, until brown.

4. Transfer steak to a cutting board and let rest 10 minutes. Slice into thin strips.

To make the shrimp:

1. Rinse shrimp, then dry with a paper towel.

2. Place shrimp in a bowl and add Cajun seasoning. Toss to coat.

3. Heat ½ tablespoon vegetable oil in the same skillet over medium heat. Once hot, add shrimp, season with a pinch of salt and black pepper, and cook, stirring occasionally, for 3 to 4 minutes, until opaque.

4. Remove shrimp to a plate.

To make the nachos:

1. Preheat oven to 400°F.

2. Layer half the tortilla chips on a sheet pan. Sprinkle half the cheese over the chips.

3. Sprinkle half the tomatoes, jalapeños, and red onions over the chips.

4. Season with a pinch of salt and black pepper.

5. Add another layer of chips, cheese, tomatoes, jalapeños, and red onions on top of the first layer. Season with remaining salt and black pepper.

6. Bake for 10 minutes, or until cheese has fully melted.

7. Remove the nachos from oven. Top one side with the shrimp and the other side with the steak.

8. Garnish with green onions and diced avocado and serve.

KAILEY HOPKINS

Growing up in a sleepy little beach town, AG's first California girl Kailey Hopkins sees life as sea life and is willing to rock the boat to save it. Living in Southern California's year-round sunshine, the blonde Girl of the Year of 2003 spends her free time snorkeling in her pink and purple wetsuit, riding the waves on her silver starfish boogie board, and observing the creatures in the tide pools with her golden retriever Sandy. She successfully protests a new building development with her best friend, keeping the integrity of the oceanside cliff intact.

Hang Ten Cocktail and Mocktail

JOSS KENDRICK,
Girl of the Year 2020

**MAKES 1 DRINK/
COCKTAILS AND MOCKTAILS**

This coconut rum drink is like a day at Huntington Beach—Joss's hometown. Pineapple and orange juices are sunshine in a glass, and the slow pour of blue curacao creates rolling waves at the bottom. Now that's something to cheer about!

INGREDIENTS

1½ ounces coconut rum, for cocktail

2 ounces orange juice

2 ounces pineapple juice

1½ ounces cream of coconut, for mocktail

1 ounce blue curacao (alcoholic or nonalcoholic)*

RECIPE STEPS

1. In a tall or hurricane glass with ice, pour in rum, orange juice, and pineapple juice. For the mocktail, substitute cream of coconut for the rum. Stir.

2. Hold the glass in one hand and slightly tip it while pouring blue curacao slowly down the side. Blue waves should fill the bottom! Shred that drink!

*Nonalcoholic blue curacao is generally available in stores that specialize in selling spirits.

JOSS KENDRICK

Surfer girl Joss Kendrick is all in, 100 percent. Joss has hearing loss but that doesn't stop her from doing the things she loves—and 2020's Girl of the Year is never happier than when she's catching waves on her Ombré shortboard with best friend Sofia and her surfing English bulldog, Murph. But when Joss joins the cheer squad on a dare, it threatens to wipe out her friendship with Sofia. Joss builds a friendship as sturdy as a cheer pyramid with fellow cheerleader Brooklyn, making Sofia feel left behind. When Sofia realizes that Joss's cheer moves are helping her surf skills, she embraces Joss's new sport and her new friends—giving American Girl fans two sports collections to enjoy!

Ski Slope Fry

GWYNN TAN,
Sister of Corinne Tan,
Girl of the Year 2022

MAKES 6 SERVINGS/ APPETIZERS AND SNACKS

Many kids learn to ski with a hunger-inducing lesson: slide downhill by positioning skis parallel to look like french fries, and slow down by pushing the heels apart and the tips of the skis together to form a pizza slice shape. As the daughters of an Aspen ski coach, Gwynn and older sister Corinne Tan probably heard this dozens of times! This classic instruction is transformed into a saucy, salty culinary chomp that's the perfect way to close out your day's romp.

INGREDIENTS

1 24-ounce jar marinara sauce

4 ounces pepperoni, diced into ¼-inch chunks

4 cups vegetable oil

2 russet potatoes

1 teaspoon salt

½ teaspoon garlic salt, divided

½ cup shredded mozzarella cheese

¼ cup sliced cherry tomatoes

¼ teaspoon red pepper flakes

1 teaspoon thinly sliced fresh basil, for garnish

RECIPE STEPS

1. Preheat oven to 425°F.
2. Heat marinara in a small pot over medium heat and bring to a simmer.
3. Sear pepperoni chunks in a small nonstick skillet over medium heat for 4 minutes, tossing regularly.
4. Heat vegetable oil in a large deep skillet over medium-high heat until it reaches 375°F.
5. Peel and slice potatoes into ½-inch strips.
6. Fry potatoes in vegetable oil for 5 minutes, until browned, mixing regularly. When done, transfer to paper-towel-lined plate. Season with salt and a pinch of garlic salt.
7. Transfer potatoes into a 13 x 9-inch baking dish. Top with mozzarella, marinara sauce, cherry tomatoes, and pepperoni. Season with remaining garlic salt and red pepper flakes.
8. Put into oven for 5 minutes.
9. Remove from oven and top with sliced basil. Serve immediately.

GWYNN TAN

At seven years old, Gwynn Tan is a little sister who confidently embraces life. She is excited about all the opportunities change presents: a new stepfather, a new baby brother, and a new sport—ice skating.

The Tan sisters are tight, sharing a bedroom, "a sister brain," as Gwynn calls their sisterly intuition, and a passion for skiing. Their dad is a ski instructor who teaches them to improve their skills on the slopes.

RED

CHAPTER 4

Entertaining Eats

There were times when we wouldn't go anywhere without our dolls—dance class, band practice, art class. And why not? They are our biggest fans! Talent can be realized at any age, but the preteen years are when many creatives discover their interests and abilities—and American Girl gave us the characters, stories, wardrobes, and playsets to be courageous and confident in exploring all kinds of creative expression.

Whether writing songs like Tenney, singing to bring people together like Melody, or acting in a movie like Rebecca, these girls know how to put on a show. Before a concert, during an art show or a karaoke night, or at an after-party for a dance performance or poetry reading, lay out this spread by the speakers!

Deli Delight

REBECCA RUBIN,
Historical Character 1914

MAKES 4 SERVINGS/ APPETIZERS AND SNACKS

The Reuben and the pastrami on rye are two Jewish American classic deli sandwiches. Although Rebecca probably wouldn't have eaten them (she is kosher!*), these sandwiches tell the story of and celebrate the Jewish deli tradition in New York City. One legend of the development of the Reuben sandwich begins in 1914, the same year Rebecca Rubin's story begins. But the connections don't stop there! As the story goes, Annette Seelos, a struggling silent film performer who was cast in a Charlie Chaplin film, stopped at Reuben's, the Manhattan restaurant the stars flocked to after the Broadway shows let out. The beautiful actress asked for a free sandwich, and restaurateur Arnold Reuben cobbled together what he had available: ham, cheese, turkey, sauerkraut, and dressing. Initially named after Seelos, sparking the trend of food named after celebrities, the meats and toppings on the sandwich eventually changed, as did the name.

INGREDIENTS

1 cup sauerkraut, drained
1 tablespoon extra-virgin olive oil
1 pound corned beef (or pastrami), sliced
4 individual-sized challah bread rolls, sliced horizontally in half (you can also use rye bread instead)
2 tablespoons unsalted butter, softened
½ cup Russian dressing
8 slices baby Swiss cheese
1 teaspoon poppy seeds

RECIPE STEPS

1. If using, turn on and preheat a panini press.
2. Add sauerkraut to a fine mesh strainer and squeeze out all liquid. Pat dry with paper towels. Set aside.
3. Heat olive oil over medium heat in a medium skillet. Add corned beef and cook each side for 45 seconds. Remove from the skillet and set aside.
4. Spread the top and bottom of each challah roll with butter. Open each roll face up and spread Russian dressing on the open face of each roll.
5. Place a Swiss cheese slice on top of the Russian dressing on each slice of the challah roll.
6. Add one-quarter of the corned beef and one-quarter of the sauerkraut on top of half the dressing and cheese-topped challah slices, then top with the remaining challah slices to form the sandwich.
7. Place the sandwich onto the panini press and press down for 1 minute per sandwich. If not using a panini press, heat same skillet over medium heat and cook both sides of each sandwich for 2 minutes or until golden-brown.
8. Top with poppy seeds and serve.

*For those who are kosher, please skip the butter, cheese, and Russian dressing (or substitute dressing with mustard). Seek out kosher-certified ingredients.

REBECCA RUBIN

Pretty in plum dresses and velvet shoes, Rebecca Rubin, the first Jewish American Historical Character, takes on the changes of the early twentieth century by storm! Living in New York City in 1914, where entertainment is thriving, Rebecca Rubin turns her love of acting into action. When she learns Jewish immigrants are fleeing persecution in Russia, including Cousin Ana, Rebecca puts out a hat and puts on a street performance to raise money for Ana's safe passage to the United States. Rebecca's spark grows and so does her stage: she plays a role in a silent movie, gives a speech to protest terrible factory conditions, and saves Ana from a broken Ferris wheel at Coney Island.

Nashville Waylon' Hot Chicken

TENNEY GRANT,
Contemporary Character 2017

**MAKES 8 TENDERS/
MAIN MUNCHIES**

Best-Ever Chicken Tenders is a legacy menu item for the American Girl Café. This version brings the heat, inspired by Georgia's Genuine Tennessee Hot Chicken, the food truck owned by Tenney's chef mom. It's guaranteed to be a hit!

INGREDIENTS

2 large eggs

2 cups plus 1 tablespoon buttermilk, divided

2 tablespoons hot sauce

¼ cup dill pickle juice

2 boneless chicken breasts, cut into 4 pieces each

3 cups all-purpose flour

4 tablespoons kosher salt, divided

3 tablespoons plus 1 teaspoon cayenne pepper, divided

1 tablespoon garlic powder

1½ teaspoons smoked paprika

2 tablespoons honey

1 teaspoon red pepper flakes

3 tablespoons light brown sugar, lightly packed

4 cups vegetable oil

8 Hawaiian rolls

8 dill pickle slices

RECIPE STEPS

To make the buttermilk dredge:

1. In a large bowl, whisk eggs, 2 cups buttermilk, hot sauce, and pickle juice.

2. Add chicken and turn to coat.

3. Cover and refrigerate for 4 hours or overnight.

To make the flour dredge:

1. Combine flour, 2 tablespoons salt, 1 teaspoon cayenne pepper, and 1 tablespoon buttermilk.

2. Whisk.

To make the chicken:

1. Mix remaining cayenne pepper, garlic powder, smoked paprika, 1½ tablespoons salt, honey, red pepper flakes, and brown sugar in a medium heatproof bowl. Set aside.

2. Preheat oven to 200°F

3. Fill a large heavy-bottomed pot with vegetable oil and heat to 350°F.

4. Dunk each piece of chicken into the flour dredge. Toss to fully cover.

5. Add half the chicken pieces to the hot oil. Turning occasionally, cook 10 minutes or until chicken registers an internal temperature of 165°F.

6. Transfer chicken to a wire rack set over a rimmed baking sheet. Season with remaining salt and keep warm in preheated oven.

7. Cook second batch of chicken, following steps 4 to 6.

8. Pour 1 cup of the hot frying oil into the bowl with the spice mixture. Whisk.

9. Once thoroughly mixed, toss each piece of chicken in the spicy oil, then return chicken to the wire rack over a rimmed baking sheet. Pour remaining spicy oil over the chicken pieces.

10. Serve chicken in a sliced Hawaiian roll with a pickle slice.

TENNEY GRANT

Singer-songwriter Tenney Grant follows her inner star, even after her musical mom and dad put the brakes on her music career. After impressing the head of Mockingbird Records, she signs with a manager for development, who pairs her with drummer Logan Everett (American Girl's first boy doll).

Tenney feels protective over the songs she writes but soon learns what Nashville is known for: collaboration! Nashville songwriters thrive when writing and jamming with other musicians.

Pop Motion Spotcorn

Z YANG,
Contemporary Character 2017

**MAKES 4 BOWLS/
APPETIZERS AND SNACKS**

Suzanne "Z" Yang has many passions—filmmaking, vlogging, her hometown of Seattle—but topping the list is her dalmatian, Popcorn! Her adorable four-legged friend earned his name because of his high energy, jumping up like hot kernels and popping in every direction. And like fresh popcorn, he brings you a burst of happiness. Here, we pay respect to Popcorn with a snack he'll slobber for: sweet popcorn with black and white spots and a hint of bacon flavoring. It's perfect for creative sessions with friends or watching your favorite films and shows. Yip-yip-yippee!

INGREDIENTS

6 strips bacon
¾ cup popcorn kernels
4 tablespoons salted butter
2 tablespoons maple syrup
Salt, to taste
Black pepper, to taste

RECIPE STEPS

1. In a large pot over medium heat, cook bacon slices until crispy.
2. When done, remove the pot from heat. Place bacon to cool on paper towels. When cool enough to handle, crumble bacon into bits and set aside.
3. Leave bacon grease in the pot. Return the pot to the burner; set again to medium heat.
4. Add popcorn kernels and cover with a lid. Shake the pot to stir up the kernels. Once popping slows, remove from heat.
5. Place butter and maple syrup in a separate saucepan and heat on low, stirring until warm and the butter is melted. Once heated, stir in the bacon bits.
6. Layer popcorn and syrupy topping into a large, clean paper bag. Shake hard to coat.
7. Pour into individual bowls. Sprinkle salt and black pepper to taste.

Z YANG

Digital content creator Suzanne "Z" Yang can always be counted on to bring Popcorn to the show! The Contemporary Character's dog is her constant companion while filming American Girl stop-motion videos and her documentary exploring her hometown from her point of view, cleverly titled *Zeattle*. Not only did Z give us the first Korean American contemporary doll with her own storyline *and* an awesome director's playset with a cute clapperboard, but she also gave us a life lesson for adulthood: if you love what you do, and you do it with friends, it's not work!

To Beat or Not to Beet Salad

GABRIELA McBRIDE,
Girl of the Year 2017

MAKES 4 SERVINGS/ SIDES AND SALADS

As a dancer and a poet, Gabriela McBride's got the beat—comfortable expressing herself in both art forms when she's at the Liberty Arts Center. Full of antioxidants, this healthy salad will keep your toes tapping through any performance. Yep, Gabriela's got the "beet," and balancing out the root vegetable's earthiness with the lightness of the pear is pure poetry.

INGREDIENTS

3 medium beets

½ cup extra-virgin olive oil, divided

1 teaspoon salt, divided

1 teaspoon black pepper, divided

2 tablespoons sherry vinegar

1 tablespoon honey

4 cups arugula

2 pears, peeled and cut into ½-inch slices

¼ cup feta cheese

¼ cup pecans, chopped

RECIPE STEPS

To make the beets:

1. Preheat oven to 375°F.
2. Clean beets well, trim top and bottom of each, peel, then chop into 2-inch pieces.
3. Place beets in a baking dish and toss with ¼ cup olive oil, ¼ teaspoon salt, and ¼ teaspoon black pepper.
4. Cover the dish with a lid or foil and bake for 40 minutes, or until beets are fork tender.
5. Let beets cool, then cut into ½-inch slices.

To make the salad:

1. Prepare the vinaigrette: in a small bowl, combine ¼ cup olive oil, sherry vinegar, honey, ½ teaspoon salt, and ½ teaspoon black pepper. Whisk to combine.
2. In a large bowl, add the arugula, roasted beets, pears, feta cheese, and pecans. Season with the remaining salt and black pepper.
3. Toss with the vinaigrette and serve.

GABRIELA McBRIDE

When the Liberty Arts Center's electrical system goes on the fritz, needing expensive repairs, a fundraising effort is put into motion by 2017's American Girl with the fabulous curls. Pleas for support means public speaking, and Gabby, who has a stutter, uses smart strategies to fundraise: she speaks slowly and acts fast, creating a dance and poetry fundraising performance in the park that goes viral. When she runs for student council, she taps into her skill set and raps her campaign speech, giving a showstopping performance!

Not a Queen Cupcake

CÉCILE REY,
Historical Character 1853

MAKES 15 CUPCAKES/ SWEETS AND DESSERTS

No matter that her parrot Cochon squawks "Not a queen, not a queen!," Cécile Rey is definitely royalty. Coming from a prominent New Orleans family, she looks forward to the festivities surrounding the city's most famous celebration, Mardi Gras. This cupcake recipe is inspired by king cake, a pastry that brings together the historical, cultural, and culinary traditions of Mardi Gras. The baked good is more than a sweet treat; it's a treasure hunt—a tiny baby doll is hidden inside the cake, and the person who finds the baby hidden in their slice gets to be king or queen for a day.

This fluffy adaptation of king cake is ideal for Mardi Gras celebrations, as well as birthday parties, baby showers, and any event where you need to feed many guests and want to use different fillings or play a game by hiding a trinket. Instead of the traditional bread texture associated with Fat Tuesday, Mardi Gras is represented visually with its vivid colors in the cake and the topping. The frosting is whipped until it's as light as a cloud—a bite tastes like a rainbow! Cinnamon and cream cheese are flavors associated with king cake, but fruit puree, lemon curd, jam, Nutella, and marshmallow fluff can be used, if preferred.

Six bowls will be needed for creating three different colors of batter and three different colors of frosting.

INGREDIENTS

Vanilla cupcakes

¾ cup salted butter

1⅔ cups all-purpose flour

1 cup sugar

¼ teaspoon baking soda

1¼ teaspoons baking powder

3 egg whites, room temperature

2 teaspoons vanilla extract

¼ cup sour cream

½ cup whole milk

Food coloring, green, yellow, and purple (or blue and red, to mix)

Cinnamon cream cheese filling

4 ounces (½ package) cream cheese, softened

⅛ cup granulated sugar

¼ teaspoon ground cinnamon

½ teaspoon vanilla extract

Buttercream frosting

1¼ cups unsalted butter, softened to room temperature

2½ cups powdered sugar

⅛ cup heavy or whipping cream

1 teaspoon pure vanilla extract

Food coloring, green, yellow, and purple

Toppings of your choice, such as sanding sugar, sparkle sugar, and sprinkles (purple, green, and yellow or gold)

RECIPE STEPS

To make the cupcakes:

1. Melt butter and set aside to cool.

2. Preheat oven to 350°F. Line a 12-cup muffin pan and half of a 6-cup muffin pan with cupcake liners.

3. In a large bowl, whisk flour, sugar, baking soda, and baking powder.

4. Add egg whites, vanilla extract, sour cream, and milk. Using an electric mixer, beat on medium speed until smooth. Gradually mix in butter.

5. Divide batter into three bowls. Into one bowl, stir in drops of green food coloring until the color is vivid. Repeat with yellow food coloring in another bowl, and purple food coloring in the third.

6. Using a spoon, drop each color batter into each cup of the lined cupcake pan, layering the colors and filling two-thirds full.

7. Bake 18 to 20 minutes, or until a toothpick comes out clean.

8. Allow to cool for 3 minutes before moving lined cupcakes to a wire rack to finish cooling.

To make the cinnamon cream cheese filling:

1. In a small bowl, combine cream cheese, granulated sugar, cinnamon, and vanilla extract. Beat until smooth.

2. Once cupcakes are cooled, use a cupcake or apple corer to remove the center of each cupcake.

3. Fill the center of the cupcakes with the cream cheese filling, or another filling of your choice.

4. In one cupcake, "hide the baby" by inserting a small, heat-resistant plastic baby doll into the center of the cupcake. Be sure to tell guests the game before they take a bite!

To make the buttercream frosting:

1. In another large bowl, cream softened butter until light and fluffy. While mixing on low speed, gradually add in powdered sugar until thoroughly combined.

2. Add heavy or whipping cream and vanilla extract. Mix on low speed until all is smooth, light, and airy.

3. Divide the buttercream evenly into three different bowls. Add drops of green food coloring to desired color and mix on medium high for 8 minutes. Rinse off the electric beaters and spatula and repeat the process with yellow and purple food coloring. You should now have three bowls of fluffy, colored frosting representing the colors of Mardi Gras: purple for justice, green for faith, and gold for power.

4. Frosting can be applied as desired. Frost each one a different shade and add purple, green, and yellow or gold toppings of sanding sugar, sparkle sugar, or sprinkles.

5. Or, if you are ready to create a showstopper with a tri-color swirl: Transfer the three bowls of colored buttercream into three piping bags. Prepare a fourth piping bag by fitting the nozzle of your choice onto the nose of the bag.

6. Cut off the pointy end of the other full bags and place them inside the empty fourth bag.

7. Begin icing by squeezing the bag. All three colors should emerge as a pastel stripey swirl.

8. Top cupcakes with your choice of sanding sugar, sparkle sugar, or sprinkles.

9. They're ready to serve—but remember to make sure guests are made aware that one of the cupcakes is host to the tiny doll!

CÉCILE REY

Growing up as a part of high society in New Orleans in 1853, Cécile is a *fille de couleur libre* with artistic dreams, leading a life of luxury. Wearing fine clothes, attending fancy balls, demonstrating proper etiquette, and getting a formal education in the performing arts like opera and Shakespeare, Cécile is the perfect guide to introduce newcomer Marie-Grace Gardner and American Girl fans to the magic of Mardi Gras season.

Motor Fizzy Cocktail

MELODY ELLISON,
Historical Character 1964

MAKES 1 DRINK/
COCKTAILS AND MOCKTAILS

Melody lives in Detroit, where the Motown sound is soaring, and even sings backup when her brother Dwayne and his band, The Three Ravens, are signed to the legendary label. Detroit is also called the Motor City, which is the inspiration for this effervescent twist on a Gin Rickey, created in conjunction with mixologist Olivia Sureties of Fig 19 in New York City. Add Michigan cherries for a finishing touch.

INGREDIENTS

2½ ounces gin
1 ounce lemon juice
¾ ounce simple syrup
¾ ounce egg white
¾ ounce wild black cherry juice
Club soda
Cherry on a toothpick, for garnish

RECIPE STEPS

1. In a cocktail shaker, mix gin, lemon juice, simple syrup, egg white, and wild black cherry juice. Dry shake (no ice).

2. Add ice and shake again.

3. Pour into a tall glass filled with ice. Top with club soda. Garnish by laying a cherry on a toothpick across the top of the glass.

MELODY ELLISON

Inspired by hearing Dr. Martin Luther King Jr. deliver the first iteration of his "I Have a Dream" speech, Melody Ellison realizes that words have power. Observing how activist sister Yvonne motivates her family to stand up for civil rights, Melody's epiphany is that when we raise our voices together, we create a harmony that can reach ears far and wide. Cheers to Melody with this Detroit-inspired cocktail.

Artistic Albuquerque Apricot Mojito

SAIGE COPELAND,
Girl of the Year 2013

**MAKES 4 DRINKS/
COCKTAILS AND MOCKTAILS**

Saige Copeland doesn't live in a desert; she lives in a work of art. This Albuquerque tween sees the world in terms of color and the environment around her as subjects to paint, like the watermelon-pink Sandia mountains near her home or the bright yellow hot air balloons that dot the blue-violet sky. With or without the rum, this ice-blended cooler brings the smiles, using New Mexico's famous fruit, which reflects the shade of Saige's hair and freckles under the Albuquerque sun.

INGREDIENTS

8 ripe apricots, halved and pitted
1½ cups simple syrup
1¼ cups white rum, for cocktail
2½ cups ice
12 mint leaves, 4 reserved for garnish
8 ounces club soda (optional)

RECIPE STEPS

1. Add apricots, simple syrup, rum, ice, and 8 mint leaves into a blender. For a mocktail, leave out the rum. Puree until smooth.

2. Divide into four glasses over ice. Thin out with club soda, if preferred. Garnish each with a mint leaf.

SAIGE COPELAND

When school budget cuts take art off the schedule, painter Saige Copeland can't brush it aside. Orchestrating the genius Day of Beige protest, she and friends Tessa, Gabi, and Dylan invite the media to see students coming to school dressed in the shade of blah to visually demonstrate how bland life is without art. When her clever "school-in" is a success, persuading the principal to offer art classes after school, 2013's Girl of the Year proves that creativity goes beyond the canvas.

Dancing Delight

MARISOL LUNA,
Girl of the Year 2005

MAKES 1 SHOT/
COCKTAILS AND MOCKTAILS

Marisol is an avid dancer living in a bustling Mexican American neighborhood in Chicago. She's skilled in ballet *folklórico* (a traditional Mexican folk dance) and dabbles in tap, jazz, and the most challenging for her—ballet. Although ballet is proving to be an uphill battle, neighbor and dance instructor Miss Mendoza convinces her that ballet is the foundation for many dance styles and is important to learn. Competitive Marisol takes this advice head-on and continues to work hard on her skills.

Inspired by Marisol's Mexican heritage, the colorful dress of ballet *folklórico*, and the candy stashes she likes to keep around, this version of the Mexican Candy Shot is smooth and tasty and, like Miss Mendoza, will have you dancing all day and night.

INGREDIENTS

Chamoy sauce, for rim

Tajin, for rim

1½ teaspoons lemon juice, freshly squeezed

1 ounce mezcal

½ ounce watermelon pucker or watermelon schnapps

¼ ounce agave nectar

Dash of the hottest hot sauce you can find

RECIPE STEPS

1. Line chamoy sauce on the rim of an empty shot glass. Dust the rim with tajin.

2. Pour lemon juice into a mixing glass.

3. Add mezcal, watermelon pucker or schnapps, agave nectar, and hot sauce. Stir.

4. Pour into a rimmed shot glass. Pucker up!

MARISOL LUNA

We meet the first Mexican American Girl of the Year in Marisol Luna in October 2005, when she finds out her family is moving from their Chicago apartment into the suburbs. The new house is fancy (the bathtub has six jets!), but Marisol enters panic mode when she learns Des Plaines does not have a dance studio, and even if the town did, it's unlikely it would teach ballet *folklórico*. Reading between the lines, it's not just Mexican dance Marisol feels she is leaving behind, it's the connection to her culture. Marisol, though, concocts a scheme to bring her heritage and her tap shoes with her, convincing upstairs neighbor Miss Mendoza to also move to Des Plaines and teach dance.

Nurture
NATURE
AMERICA'S NATIONAL PARK

CHAPTER 5

Girls Trip

When you had to pack for a road trip, there was no way you were forgetting your doll. Or your American Girl books. Or movies. She was there to keep you company and adventure with you! American Girls thrive in their travels, and these dolls introduced the wonder of the rest of the world to us. Girls of the Year see the sights in exciting locations or, in Kanani's case, reside on an island paradise where others come to visit! Whether you and your besties are traveling by road, rail, ship, or air, these drinks and light bites turn a trip into a treat worth exploring.

Monkey Acai, Monkey Do Brazilian Bowl

LEA CLARK,
Girl of the Year 2016

MAKES 2 BOWLS/
APPETIZERS AND SNACKS

When Lea Clark travels to Brazil, things get wild! In her movie *Lea to the Rescue*, she brazenly follows poachers into the jungle, running ahead of her babysitter and brother's girlfriend, Paloma, who has no choice but to follow. Though the two get lost, they have a mesmerizing adventure. Discovered by a tweenage Indigenous Amazonian, Lea and Paloma are brought to the tribe's tropical village, which inspired the Rainforest House playset that allowed imaginations to fly faster than a harpy eagle. Another awesome inclusion to Lea's collection was an Acai Bowl and Fruit Smoothie Stand. Lea's trip to Brazil also brought her face-to-face with incredible wildlife, and this healthy, delicious snack celebrates her love for animals and Brazil's tropical fruits. It's so quick and easy even Lea's three-toed sloth could make it in minutes.

INGREDIENTS

2 frozen bananas, peeled and sliced before freezing

⅔ cup coconut water, nondairy milk, pineapple juice, or apple juice, divided

1 cup frozen acai cubes or two 3½-ounce frozen acai packets, broken into smaller pieces

1 cup frozen strawberries, tops removed before freezing

½ cup frozen blueberries

⅓ cup peanut butter (optional)

¼ cup honey (if using unsweetened acai packets)

Suggested toppings

Blueberries
Raspberries
Bananas, sliced
Strawberries, sliced
Mango, sliced
Kiwi, sliced
Granola
Cocoa nibs
Coconut flakes
Honey, for drizzling

RECIPE STEPS

1. Hours before preparing the bowls, freeze bananas. Other fruits do not need to be frozen that far ahead of time. (All of these fruits, including bananas, can be purchased already frozen at the grocery store.)

2. Before removing the frozen fruit from the freezer, make and plate a spread of sliced fresh fruit and other toppings.

3. Into a powerful blender, pour in ⅓ cup liquid (coconut water, milk, or juice). Add the frozen fruit (bananas, acai, strawberries, blueberries) and peanut butter, if desired. If necessary, add honey.

4. Blend until smooth. If necessary to soften, add more of the liquid, a teaspoon at a time. If chunky objects are getting stuck, turn off the blender and stir with a wooden spoon or tamper, pushing frozen items to bottom of blender. If it's not solid enough, thicken by adding more sliced frozen bananas. If it's still too thin, pour into a bowl and place in the freezer for 20 minutes. (Alternate choice: pour into a tall glass and drink because now it's a smoothie!)

5. Spoon into bowls. Top with your choice of fruit, granola, and other toppings. Drizzle with honey. Eat up!

LEA CLARK

When Girl of the Year 2016 Lea Clark leaves St. Louis to visit older brother Zac at his internship at a wildlife sanctuary in South America, she takes American Girl fans on a Brazilian bonanza. Camera in hand, Lea is just hoping to see some wildlife to snap. But there's no time to monkey around: instead, she meets a new friend, conquers her fear of the ocean, canoes down the Amazon, and rescues both her injured father from the side of a cliff and an injured baby sloth from the floor of the rainforest.

Blue Hawai'i Cocktail

NANEA MITCHELL,
Historical Character 1941

**MAKES 1 DRINK/
COCKTAILS AND MOCKTAILS**

One of the most delicious details from Nanea's story is her love for shaved ice. Not only is it Nanea's favorite treat, it's also loved by Kanani, Girl of the Year 2011, who lives in Kaua'i. Each doll has her own adorable shaved ice stand playset. The Blue Hawai'i Cocktail is imbued with the soothing color of the subtropical Pacific, combined with the spirits of aloha: pineapple and rum.

INGREDIENTS

3 ounces pineapple juice

½ ounce simple syrup

½ ounce lime juice, freshly squeezed

½ ounce blue curacao (alcoholic or nonalcoholic)*

¾ ounce vodka, for cocktail

¾ ounce light or coconut rum, for cocktail

1 ounce cream of coconut, for mocktail

Pineapple slice, for garnish

Orchid, for garnish

RECIPE STEPS

1. In a tall glass with ice, pour ingredients in this order: pineapple juice, simple syrup, lime juice, blue curacao, vodka, and rum. Stir. For the mocktail, substitute the vodka and rum with cream of coconut and use nonalcoholic blue curacao.

2. Garnish with a pineapple slice or orchid.

*Nonalcoholic blue curacao is generally available in stores that specialize in selling spirits.

NANEA MITCHELL

Historical Character and Native Hawaiian Nanea Mitchell is living in paradise with her *'ohana*. She spends her days attending hula lessons with Tutu, stocking the shelves in Tutu Kane's convenience store, and trying to win a contest with best friends Lily Suda and Donna Hill, who adorably call themselves the Three Kittens. Unfortunately, Nanea and her friends are living during a tumultuous time in history, experiencing the bombing of Pearl Harbor, which pulls the United States into World War II. Nanea's dog, Mele, is a big source of comfort for her at this time.

Shrimp on the Bailey

KIRA BAILEY,
Girl of the Year 2021

MAKES 4 SERVINGS/ APPETIZERS AND SNACKS

When Kira and her mother arrive at the Bailey Wildlife Refuge in Australia, they observe that caring for the animal residents is wonderful but a lot of work! Everyone lives, works, and dines together at the sanctuary, doing double duty when necessary. For example, Kira meets large animal handler Mr. Curry and his daughter, Alexis, when they're rounding 'roos; a few hours later, she learns he's also the sanctuary's chef when he welcomes the new guests with a delicious dinner of barbecued prawns. Inspired by Mr. Curry's resourceful meal, all the ingredients for this delectable dish are native to Australia. While it cannot be made on the cutie AG toy barbecue set (future idea, Mattel!), it is easily made on an indoor grill and is ideal for a campout.

INGREDIENTS

⅓ cup unsalted butter

1 clove garlic, minced

2 limes, juice and zest, divided

⅓ cup extra-virgin olive oil

1½ pounds uncooked shrimp, deveined

Salt and black pepper, to taste

2 tablespoons fresh cilantro, chopped

1 red chili pepper, seeded and finely chopped, for garnish

RECIPE STEPS

1. Melt butter in a small saucepan over low heat. Stir in garlic, all the lime juice, and zest of one lime. Remove from heat.

2. Heat olive oil in a large nonstick skillet over medium heat. When hot, add shrimp. Season with salt and black pepper. Cook for 3 to 4 minutes, turning often, until shrimp become slightly pink and opaque. Remove from heat.

3. Plate shrimp and top with the butter-lime mixture and cilantro.

4. Garnish with chili pepper and remaining lime zest.

5. Serve immediately.

KIRA BAILEY

Kira Bailey and her mother head to Australia for the summer. Arriving at her aunt Mamie and aunt Lynette's wildlife sanctuary, she's excited to learn that she gets to stay in a dreamy platform tent that defines the word "glamping." Kira is an aspiring veterinarian herself, and while she's a little worried about the funnel-web spiders and poisonous snakes that reside in the bush, she's overjoyed to cuddle and feed koala joey Bean, supervise wombats Boomer and Daisy's playtime, and work with ornithology graduate student Evie to investigate a mysterious bird that just might be the paradise parrot, believed to be extinct!

Raspberry Beret Soufflé

GRACE THOMAS,
Girl of the Year 2015

MAKES 6 SERVINGS/ SWEETS AND DESSERTS

Through Grace, we all get to go to Paris! She bikes along past the Seine, the Eiffel Tower, and the Palace of Versailles, all while enjoying double-scoop ice cream cones and exploring with adorable stray French bulldog Bonbon. Most relevant, she takes us behind the scenes of a French patisserie, learns to speak French, and never, as Grace learns, sweeps while baking.

The *Grace Stirs Up Success* movie takes us down even more fantastic *rues*! The film's third act is all about Grace as a fictional contestant on *MasterChef Junior*, a reality competition TV series everyone was watching in 2015. And finally, the throughline is Grace's attempts to make the soufflé. She accomplishes this while looking the absolute cutest in her polka dots, bows, and French-themed clothing line. So put on your raspberry-colored beret because if a fictional ten-year-old can do it, so can you!

INGREDIENTS

Raspberry puree

2 cups fresh or frozen raspberries

½ cup granulated sugar

1¼ tablespoons lemon or lime juice

Soufflé

1 tablespoon unsalted butter, melted, for greasing

3½ tablespoons granulated sugar, divided

5 large egg whites, room temperature

¼ teaspoon cream of tartar

1 cup raspberry puree

Powdered sugar, for dusting

Raspberries, for garnish

RECIPE STEPS

To make the raspberry puree:

1. In a small saucepan, combine raspberries, sugar, and lemon or lime juice. Set to medium heat and bring to a boil.

2. Stir, gently breaking apart raspberries, for about 6 to 9 minutes until it starts to thicken. Remove from heat.

3. Strain through a fine mesh sieve to remove seeds. Use a spoon to press fruit through the sieve.

4. Set 1 cup of puree aside and let cool. Store any remainder in the refrigerator for future use, such as an ice cream topping.

To make the soufflé:

1. Preheat oven to 375°F. Place a baking sheet on the middle rack of oven.

2. Brush melted butter into ramekins. Use 1 tablespoon granulated sugar to coat ramekins evenly. Shake out excess sugar.

3. In a large bowl, whisk egg whites until soft peaks form. If using an electric mixer with a whisk accessory, keep at a low speed until foamy, then slowly increase speed.

4. Add cream of tartar and continue to whisk as peaks become firmer. Slowly whisk in remaining 2½ tablespoons of sugar until stiff, glossy peaks form.

5. Aggressively fold one-quarter of the egg whites into the raspberry puree. Then, gently fold in half of the remaining egg whites into puree. Fold in the remainder of the egg whites with even more delicacy, using care to keep mixture fluffy.

6. Gently pour or spoon batter into ramekins, filling to the top, and taking care not to spill over onto rims. If necessary, use a small paper towel to clean rims.

7. Place ramekins on the preheated baking sheet. Bake for 15 to 17 minutes until they've fully risen and are just golden-brown. Do not open oven to check on the soufflé's progress!

8. Dust with powdered sugar. Place one raspberry on top of each, for garnish. Serve immediately and give yourself a chef's kiss!

Menu
La Pâtisserie
Chocolate Cupcake $ 4
Strawberry Tart $ 3
Baguette $ 2
La Pâtisserie
MENU

GRACE THOMAS

Grace Thomas is the Girl of the Year who truly embodies her specific year. "Girlboss" was a term on everyone's lips in 2015, and Grace is an entrepreneur who definitely embodied being a boss girl. She's an organized planner whose "my way is the best way" energy is annoying to her best friends and business partners Maddy and Ella and yet, you know, relatable. She's learning, *mes amis*, and eventually figures out how to work as a team to turn both her and her grandparents' bakeries into financial successes. This tween is going places, and luckily, we join her on her journey.

The UnBelizeable

JESS McCONNELL,
Girl of the Year 2006

MAKES 4 DRINKS/ COCKTAILS AND MOCKTAILS

The first sip of this sweet and spicy drink sparks a dawning realization: this bold cocktail is a find! While in Belize, Jess makes many discoveries: a Mayan cave, an injured baby bird Pippi, a love of kayaking, and her own courage. Jess is a true explorer, and in honor of the moment Jess realizes Belize has fire ants, enjoy this light and fruity drink that says hello with a sharp bite.

INGREDIENTS

2 red chili peppers, like Fresno or Holland

10 ounces vodka

2 ounces lime juice

1 ounce lemon juice

1 ounce orange juice

1 ounce plus 4 teaspoons simple syrup, divided

1 Granny Smith apple, peeled and finely diced, 12 pieces reserved for garnish

12 basil leaves, 8 torn, 4 reserved for garnish

RECIPE STEPS

1. At least one day before serving, slice chili peppers in half and steep them in vodka overnight.
2. To prepare the sour mix, in a small bowl combine lime juice, lemon juice, orange juice, and 1 ounce simple syrup.
3. In a large pitcher, muddle apple, torn basil, and 4 teaspoons simple syrup.
4. Add the steeped vodka and 4 ounces of the sour mix. Discard any remaining sour mix.
5. Strain half the mixture into a cocktail shaker with ice. Shake and strain into two chilled martini glasses. Repeat with remaining mixture to make two final drinks.
6. Garnish each drink with a basil leaf and 3 diced apple pieces to serve.

JESS McCONNELL

Michigander Jess McConnell may have made her debut in 2006, but she'll always be the American Cave Girl! When she goes on an archaeological dig to Belize with her family, this ten-year-old soccer player is determined to prove that the label "baby of the family" should be retired (youngest children, unite!). As her list of "firsts" grows (as in, first trip to the jungle, first time meeting a spider monkey, first visit to Mayan ruins), so does her bravery. Jess sleeps in a cave with her new Belizean friend Sarita and later discovers a sacred cave, allowing her to complete the list with first archeological discovery!

Sunset Salad

KANANI AKINA,
Girl of the Year 2011

MAKES 4 SERVINGS/ SIDES AND SALADS

There's trouble in Hawaiian paradise: Kanani and best friend Celina aren't seeing eye to eye on how to spend the summer. Kanani is working at her family's shaved ice stand to raise money for posters to educate tourists on the endangered Hawaiian monk seals who come ashore. And Celina just wants to surf, so she starts hanging out with surfer Jo, leaving paddleboarder Kanani feeling hurt and left out. When summer is nearly over, Kanani realizes that the jealousy was misplaced. Jo is like the honu turtle Tuta Lani tells her about: an unexpected friend. The girls represent the POG juices found all over the Hawaiian islands. Just like passionfruit, oranges, and guava, Kanani, Celina, and Jo are three wonderful individuals on their own, but together, they're ono-licious.

The red, orange, and yellow colors of the fruit in this salad represent the sun setting over Kaua'i, known as "the Garden Isle" for its lush greenery.

INGREDIENTS

¼ cup passionfruit juice
¼ cup orange juice
¼ cup guava juice
3 tablespoons lime juice
¼ cup extra-virgin olive oil
1 shallot, minced
¼ teaspoon salt
¼ teaspoon black pepper
3 cups chopped iceberg lettuce
1 cup sliced strawberries
1 cup chopped mango, cut into ½-inch cubes
1 orange, separated into bite-size segments
1 avocado, sliced
1 tablespoon currants
1 tablespoon chopped candied pecans

RECIPE STEPS

1. In a small bowl, stir passionfruit juice, orange juice, guava juice, lime juice, and olive oil.
2. Mix in shallot.
3. Season with salt and black pepper and set the dressing aside.
4. Place lettuce into a salad bowl.
5. On top of the lettuce, arrange strawberries, mango, oranges, and avocado.
6. Sprinkle currants and candied pecans on top of the salad.
7. Add dressing, to taste.

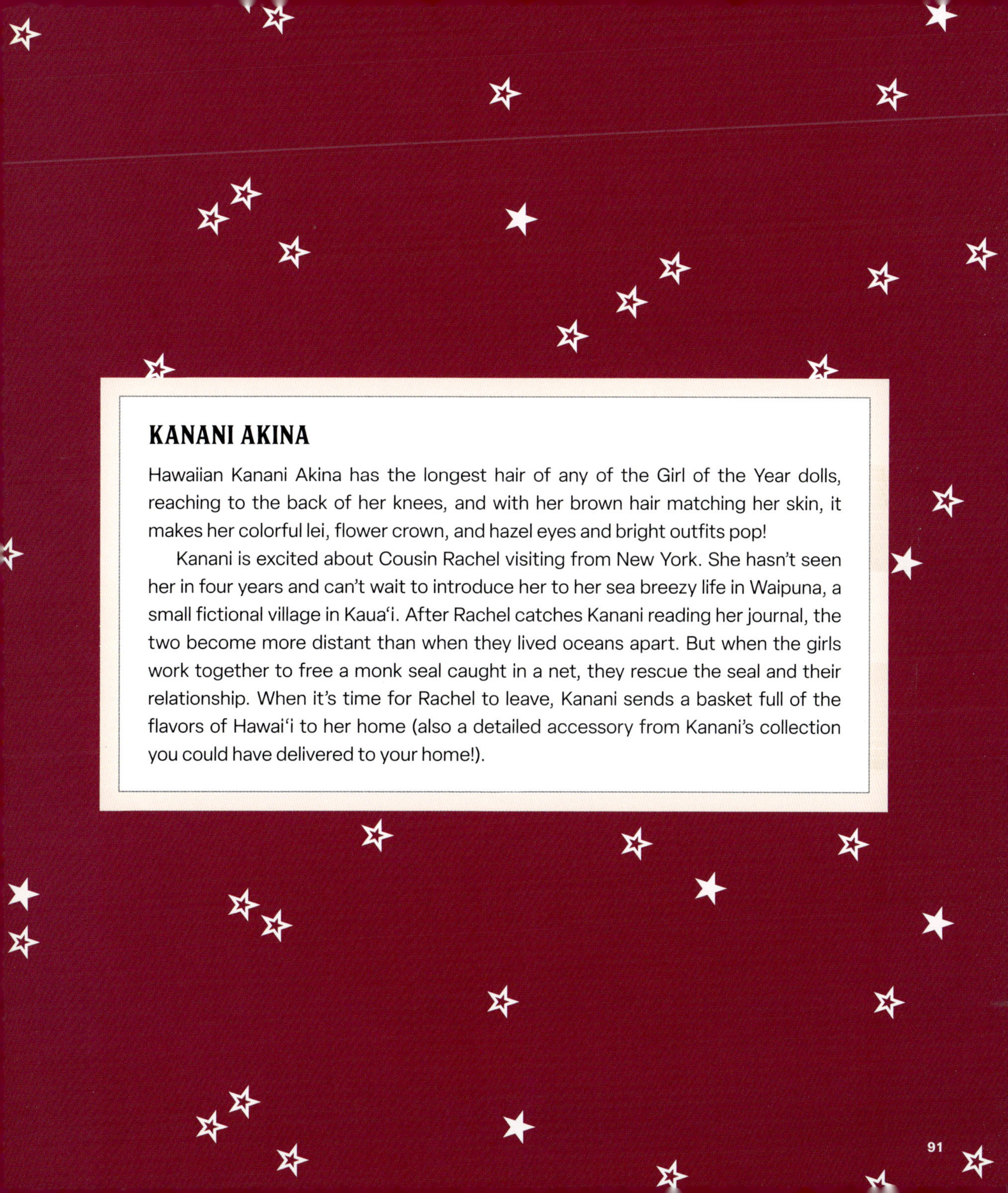

KANANI AKINA

Hawaiian Kanani Akina has the longest hair of any of the Girl of the Year dolls, reaching to the back of her knees, and with her brown hair matching her skin, it makes her colorful lei, flower crown, and hazel eyes and bright outfits pop!

Kanani is excited about Cousin Rachel visiting from New York. She hasn't seen her in four years and can't wait to introduce her to her sea breezy life in Waipuna, a small fictional village in Kaua'i. After Rachel catches Kanani reading her journal, the two become more distant than when they lived oceans apart. But when the girls work together to free a monk seal caught in a net, they rescue the seal and their relationship. When it's time for Rachel to leave, Kanani sends a basket full of the flavors of Hawai'i to her home (also a detailed accessory from Kanani's collection you could have delivered to your home!).

CHAPTER 6

Holiday Hoopla

Holidays are the best days for many kids, with special meals, activities, and family time a part of the experience—and American Girl enhanced the holiday happiness! For adult fans of American Girl, you may have excitedly flipped through the catalog when filling out your wish list and can still remember the elation of unwrapping the doll of your dreams. The joy of spending the holiday with your doll, dressing her up, and having her at the table is unmatched. And dressing her in the fantastic costumes AG offered, or perhaps making your own, and going house to house asking for candy was an absolute treat. The nostalgic joy of those days is baked into these elevated holiday recipes inspired by the dolls, perfect to share with family, friends, and the dolls in your life.

Spice Girl Cocktail and Wannabe Mocktail

ISABEL HOFFMAN,
Historical Character 1999

MAKES 6 DRINKS/ COCKTAILS AND MOCKTAILS

While the rest of the world is worrying that Y2K will bring calamity, Isabel is focused on choreography. She's leading a dance team in Seattle's Millennium Celebration, working on the perfect routine to the perfect music act—the Spice Girls, of course, whose "girl power" mantra sums up everything she wants to be! As the opening beat of this powerful drink, five-spice powder gets your palate humming. The loudest flavor is, naturally, ginger spice. The "pop" of the Champagne cork is music to the ears of your guests, and the bubbly effervescence that fills the glass swirls around an attention-getting anise star.

INGREDIENTS

Ginger simple syrup

½ cup water

½ cup chopped fresh ginger

⅔ cup sugar

Cocktail or mocktail

¼ teaspoon Chinese five-spice powder

2 tablespoons sugar

2 tablespoons chopped crystallized ginger

6 star anise

1 bottle Champagne, for cocktail

1 bottle sparkling apple cider, for mocktail

RECIPE STEPS

To make the ginger simple syrup:

1. In a small saucepan over high heat, bring water, ginger, and sugar to a boil. Once bubbles begin, lower heat to a simmer.

2. Cook until liquid is thicker, stirring occasionally, for approximately 15 minutes.

3. Remove from heat. Once cool, strain the syrup.

To make the cocktail or mocktail:

1. On a small, flat plate, combine Chinese five-spice powder and sugar. Dampen the rim of a Champagne flute with water and dip into the sugar-spice mix.

2. Drop 1 teaspoon of crystallized ginger and 1 star anise into the glass. Pour 1 tablespoon ginger simple syrup into the flute.

3. Add 3 to 4 ounces of Champagne. For the mocktail, substitute Champagne with sparkling apple cider. Cheers!

ISABEL HOFFMAN

The most memorable New Year's Eve in modern history was the closing out of the twentieth century. Sure, we partied like it was 1999, but entering a new millennium meant that the calendar on computer programs would flip over to an entirely new set of numbers: 2-0-0-0. Fear gripped the world: Would the unfamiliar digital dates mean computer chaos? Would planes plummet, electrical grids collapse, medical devices flatline, and the stock market crash? To Isabel, it seems like the end of the world has already arrived when a new girl who becomes a foil to Isabel joins her dance group, insults Isabel and Nicki's fashion style, and then kicks Isabel out of the group, taking all her friends. Isabel realizes the true meaning of "girl power" is being confident in who you are, as you are.

Hoisin Chivey

IVY LING,
Best friend of Historical Character Julie Albright from 1974

MAKES 4 SERVINGS/ MAIN MUNCHIES

Ivy's grandparents are the owners of Happy Panda, a popular Chinese restaurant in San Francisco's famed Chinatown, and their menu items waft through the stories so strongly, you can almost taste them. Many traditional Chinese dishes feature tofu as the main source of protein and star ingredient, and Ivy is a fan. This Chinese American dish will bring good luck and good health to your tummy.

INGREDIENTS

1 pound tofu*

1 cup rice

3 tablespoons hoisin sauce

3 tablespoons chili garlic sauce

2 tablespoons ketchup

2 tablespoons rice vinegar

2 tablespoons soy sauce

½ teaspoon sesame oil

1 teaspoon hot sauce

2 tablespoons water

1 tablespoon brown sugar, lightly packed

¼ teaspoon plus 3 tablespoons cornstarch, divided

¾ cup flour

2 eggs

½ teaspoon salt

¼ teaspoon black pepper

¼ teaspoon ground ginger

¼ teaspoon garlic powder

¼ teaspoon smoked paprika

4 tablespoons vegetable oil, divided

1 medium onion, chopped into ¾-inch pieces

1 red bell pepper, chopped into ¾-inch pieces

1 cup sugar snap peas, ends trimmed

2 teaspoons minced fresh ginger

4 cloves garlic, minced

¼ cup chopped chives, cut into ¼-inch pieces, for garnish

*Meat option: for tofu substitute 1 pound chicken breast, chopped into ¾-inch cubes. Increase cook time in step 7 by 1 minute.

IVY LING

Historical Character Julie Albright lovingly calls bestie Ivy Ling "Poison Ivy," and Ivy dubs Julie "Alley Oop." Ivy was released along with Julie in 2007, and she is historical in her own right. Ivy is the first Chinese American character released by American Girl with a fully developed backstory and book. Ivy is worried about doing well in school and trying to master doing a back handspring on the balance beam and finds Chinese school kind of boring. When she and Julie are preparing for the Chinese New Year, they shop for beautiful silk Chinese dresses that match their Chinese dolls, and then realize they're lost in Chinatown. Luckily, when Ivy hears the clatter of mahjong tiles, she knows her grandmother Po Po is probably near. She's right, and the family is reunited.

RECIPE STEPS

1. Press tofu between two paper towels under a heavy frying pan to release as much liquid as possible (skip this step if using chicken). Chop tofu into ¾-inch cubes.

2. Prepare rice per packaged instructions. Once completed, cover and set aside until last step.

3. In a small bowl, whisk hoisin sauce, chili garlic sauce, ketchup, rice vinegar, soy sauce, sesame oil, hot sauce, water, brown sugar, and ¼ teaspoon cornstarch. Set aside for later use.

4. Arrange a "dredging station." Use three medium shallow bowls. Fill the first bowl with flour. Fill the second with whisked eggs. Fill the third with 3 tablespoons cornstarch, salt, black pepper, ginger, garlic powder, and smoked paprika.

5. Heat 3 tablespoons vegetable oil in a large nonstick skillet over medium heat.

6. Working in batches, dredge about one-quarter of the tofu pieces in flour, then in egg, then finally in cornstarch, shaking off excess after each step.

7. Place coated tofu into the skillet. Cook until light brown, about 1 minute on each side, then remove to a paper-towel-lined plate. Repeat with remaining batches of tofu until all are coated and fried.

8. Discard oil and, once cool, wipe out skillet. In same pan, heat 1 tablespoon vegetable oil over medium-high heat.

9. Add onions and sauté for 2 minutes. Add red bell peppers, snap peas, ginger, and garlic. Cook for another minute.

10. Stir in the hoisin sauce mixture. Reduce heat to medium and simmer until sauce has thickened, about 5 minutes. Add tofu and cook for 1 minute while tossing to coat.

11. Serve over rice and garnish each serving with one-quarter of the chopped chives.

Masked Rum Balls

MARIE-GRACE GARDNER,
Historical Character 1853

MAKES 24 RUM BALLS/
SWEETS AND DESSERTS

Marie-Grace is excited to attend the Children's Opera Ball during her first Mardi Gras in New Orleans. During her time, Mardi Gras was celebrated with elegant balls, delicious feasts, and marvelous music. Today, a weeklong party culminates in brass bands performing in wild and colorful parades, where beaded necklaces are famously thrown from the floats. A hallmark that has endured through the history of Mardi Gras is the wearing of an extravagant mask, originally worn to disguise class so that revelers could mingle regardless of social hierarchy—exactly the intention of Marie-Grace and Cécile Rey, who switch masks at the Children's Ball!

Using the primary ingredient of one of New Orleans's most notable drinks, the Hurricane, these sweet grown-up treats can be dressed differently and disguise the alcohol content. The taste of the alcohol can be too harsh immediately after preparing but softens into a complex flavor that is a little sweet, a little spicy, a little chewy, and a lot of scrumptious.

INGREDIENTS

1¼ cups pecans

1 11-ounce box vanilla wafers

¾ cup confectioners' sugar

½ teaspoon salt

2 tablespoons unsweetened cocoa powder

½ cup dark rum

2 teaspoons vanilla extract

2 tablespoons light corn syrup

1 cup sugar sprinkles

RECIPE STEPS

1. Place pecans and vanilla wafers in a food processor. Pulse until ground finely into a sand-like mixture.

2. Transfer nut mixture to a large mixing bowl. Into the bowl mix confectioners' sugar, salt, and cocoa powder. Then, add rum, vanilla extract, and corn syrup and mix into a wet dough.

3. Cover the dough and chill for 30 minutes.

4. Remove from the refrigerator and roll the dough into 1-inch balls.

5. Pour sugar sprinkles onto a plate. Roll each rum ball in sprinkles to coat.

6. Refrigerate for at least 1 hour. For the best flavor, prepare the day before.

7. Serve. Or shall we say, imbibe!

MARIE-GRACE GARDNER

Moving back to her birthplace of New Orleans, shy Marie-Grace Gardner yearns for a friend. When she meets Cécile Rey, a free girl of color from a prominent family, she thinks she's spotted a bestie in the making. Cécile isn't really that into Marie-Grace—at first. Marie-Grace is shy, attends school in person, and speaks English. Cécile is bold, is homeschooled, and speaks mainly French. But even with all of their differences—societal, cultural, and racial—they're willing to make the jump and trust each other. An unlikely friendship is born. They initially meet at an opera class, and they bond over a shared love of theirs, music. Cécile slowly realizes that they have more in common than they have different. They both want to make a difference and help their community, which is evident during the strike of the deadly yellow fever—which happened in New Orleans during 1853 at this time. Although the fever interrupted their lives and impacted the ones they loved, Marie-Grace and Cécile found a way to lean on each other and their friendship to make a difference and make it through.

Wicked Good Holi-day Cookies

KAVI SHARMA,
Girl of the Year 2023

MAKES 3 DOZEN COOKIES/ SWEETS AND DESSERTS

After a winter storm blows a tree into her school's auditorium, Kavi is motivated to rent another theater for her school's production of *Annie*. A savvy problem-solver, Kavi and her friends join forces to create tie-dye tees inspired by the powders used in Holi or the Festival of Colors, celebrated by many Hindu communities each spring. Kavi bakes with her grandmother to create sugar cookies in matching shades. How sweet!

INGREDIENTS

Cookies

3 cups flour

1 teaspoon baking powder

1 teaspoon salt

1¼ cups sugar

1 cup unsalted butter, softened

2 large eggs

1½ teaspoons vanilla extract

Assortment of food coloring in the bright shades of Holi (available at craft stores or online)

Colorful sugar sprinkles

Glaze

1 cup powdered sugar

1 tablespoon light corn syrup

2 tablespoons water

KAVI SHARMA

For the first Indian American Girl of the Year, a birthday gift sets off a pivotal year in the life of Kavi Sharma—tickets to *Wicked* on Broadway! Inspired by the incredible musical numbers, the elaborate costumes, and the complex relationship between Glinda and Elphaba, Kavi starts performing on stage with her friends. First up: a Bollywood dance number in the school revue with besties Pari and Sophie. After she trips and falls during rehearsal, she's not sure she wants to get up on stage ever again. Through the support of her friends—and an amazing outfit for the Bollywood number—she decides not to quit. Persistence pays off: the dance is a hit!

RECIPE STEPS

1. In a medium bowl, stir flour, baking powder, and salt. Set aside.

2. In a large mixing bowl, beat sugar and butter until smooth.

3. Add eggs, one at a time, and vanilla extract, mixing until creamy.

4. Gradually mix in the flour mixture until the dough is stiff.

5. To prepare dye to color the dough, put drops of food coloring into small bowls. This is where the real fun begins and is a wonderful group activity with friends or little ones. Divide the dough into three or four chunks, one for each bowl of food coloring. Roll the dough chunks in the bowls. Stir the color in with a spoon or use your fingers to knead the dough until the color is soaked all the way through. Add more food coloring, if needed, so that the colors are vivid.

6. Wrap each ball of dough in a large amount of wax or parchment paper. This will be used later as a surface to roll out your dough after it chills. Put the dough balls into the freezer for 20 minutes or in the refrigerator for an hour.

7. Roll out each ball of dough on the paper it's wrapped in, having first dusted the surface of the paper with flour. Form into matching rectangles of the same size.

8. Evenly stack the dough rectangles on top of each other. Choose one of the three rectangles to be the first (bottom layer), resting on top of its parchment paper. Turn over a second rectangle so that it is parchment side up and quickly place it evenly on top of the first layer. Carefully peel the paper off. Repeat with a third layer.

9. Carefully hand-roll the rectangle stack into a tight log. Use the parchment paper on the bottom to help you roll it up, then wrap it in that paper. Freeze for 20 minutes or refrigerate for an hour (or up to two days, if you want to do this in advance).

10. Preheat oven to 350°F.

11. Line a baking sheet with parchment paper.

12. Unwrap the cookie dough log and cut off uneven ends. Slice into ⅓-inch cookies using a serrated knife and evenly space 12 on the baking sheet.

13. Bake for 8 to 10 minutes.

14. To prepare glaze, stir powdered sugar, corn syrup, and water in a bowl until smooth. While cookies are cooling, brush glaze across the tops of the cookies. Sprinkle with decorative sugar. Holi-Wow! Your friends' eyes will spin for these sweet and colorful pinwheels!

The Sweet Escake

CAROLINE ABBOTT,
Historical Character 1812

**MAKES 10 SERVINGS/
SWEETS AND DESSERTS**

Caroline's stories take place at the beginning of the War of 1812—America's second war for independence. Caroline sneaks a map to Papa to help him escape British soldiers and later discovers him injured on the route home and brings him to safety. As she watches the American flag fly gracefully above, it's a reminder that it's the simple joys that make hard-won liberty so sweet.

This light and delightful trifle inspired by the colors of the American flag is simple to make but rewarding—a perfect refreshing dessert on a hot July day.

INGREDIENTS

Angel food cake

1 cup cake flour

½ teaspoon salt

1½ cups sugar, divided

10 egg whites, room temperature

1 heaping teaspoon cream of tartar

1½ teaspoons vanilla extract

½ teaspoon almond extract

Trifle

Angel food cake, diced into cubes

4 cups vanilla yogurt, divided

2 pounds fresh strawberries, sliced

2 pints fresh blueberries

1 tub of whipped topping

RECIPE STEPS

To make the angel food cake:

1. Preheat oven to 350°F.

2. Sift flour, salt, and ¾ cup sugar, running it through the sifter three times to aerate the dry ingredients.

3. In a separate bowl, use the whisk attachment on an electric mixer to whisk egg whites, using the lowest speed. Once frothy, add cream of tartar. Increase the mixing speed to medium until soft peaks form.

4. Add vanilla and almond extracts and beat on medium. Egg whites should be glossy.

5. Gradually, whisk in remaining sugar, approximately 1 tablespoon at a time. Then, whisk on high until stiff peaks form, which should be 4 to 5 minutes.

6. Once the stiff peaks are achieved, use a spatula to slowly fold in the flour-sugar mixture. Be careful to maintain the airy fluff in the egg whites.

7. Once combined completely, gently pour into a 10-inch ungreased tube pan.

8. Place pan on center rack of oven, with room for the cake to rise.

9. Bake for approximately 40 minutes. Remove from oven when the top is golden-brown and a toothpick comes out clean.

10. Place upside down on a cooling rack or hang upside down over the top of a longneck bottle. It must cool upside down and completely to get the springy texture. Let cool for 2 to 3 hours before preparing for the trifle.

11. To remove from pan, slide in a plastic knife along the sides to loosen until the cake pops out. Using a serrated knife so as not to squish the airy cake together, cut the cake into cubes.

To make the trifle:

1. Line the bottom of a trifle dish with cubed angel food cake (homemade is much tastier than store-bought, but do what you need to do).

2. Spread half of the yogurt across the top of the cake.

3. Layer strawberries evenly across yogurt. Layer blueberries on top of strawberries.

4. Spread whipped topping evenly across blueberries.

5. Repeat the layering process, starting again with the cake: a layer of yogurt, a layer of strawberries, a layer of blueberries, followed by whipped topping, and so on. Some trifle dishes will allow for three layers; wider ones will only accommodate two.

6. The top layer of the trifle will be arranged a little differently. This time, put whipped topping on after strawberries, then finish with blueberries on top, in the shape of a large star. Or, using more strawberries, assemble with blueberries to look like an American flag.

7. Cover with plastic wrap and chill in the refrigerator for at least 4 hours before serving.

CAROLINE ABBOTT

Historical Character Caroline Abbott learns America has entered the War of 1812 the hard way: from the British soldiers who abscond with the family sloop and take her dad as a prisoner of war. But in the face of adversity, Caroline and the women rally. Caroline thinks outside the hat box to solve real-world problems, all while rocking her signature long, blonde curls and empire waist dresses. Whether she's embroidering secret maps of escape routes, creating a new hack to shoot tiny cannonballs out of a too-big cannon, or sinking her own skiff to save war supplies, Caroline shows that sometimes winning battles is a mix of slapdash strategy and action.

Sweet and Salty Sibling Treats

MOLLY McINTIRE,
Historical Character 1944

MAKES 24 SQUARES/ SWEETS AND DESSERTS

It's Halloween when we first "Meet Molly," and her costume daydreaming is interrupted when Mrs. Gilford, the family housekeeper, serves her mashed turnips—to Molly's horror. It's actually the perfect October vegetable: the original jack-o'-lanterns were carved from turnips!

After much deliberation, Molly and her best friends Linda and Susan walk through their neighborhood dressed as hula dancers, wearing grass skirts crafted from newspaper. Returning home with bags brimming with treats, Molly's annoying brother Ricky plays a mean trick: he drenches them with a garden hose, ruining their costumes and candy. As Molly and Ricky's relationship gets saltier, a revenge plot is set into motion—and then, just like the Rice Krispie treats that were popular in 1944, things get sticky in the McIntire household.

Inspired by Mrs. McIntire's hack to gussy up turnips with a small amount of sweetness, here's a trick that will make a classic Halloween treat seem like a gourmet goody.

INGREDIENTS

½ cup salted butter

1 tablespoon light corn syrup

¼ cup milk

½ cup brown sugar, packed

2 teaspoons Maldon sea salt, divided

1 10-ounce bag mini marshmallows

6 cups crispy rice cereal (like Rice Krispies)

Black and orange sprinkles (optional)

RECIPE STEPS

1. In a large pot, melt butter with corn syrup, milk, and brown sugar over low heat until butter is melted, for 6 to 8 minutes.
2. Stir in 1 teaspoon sea salt and remove from heat.
3. Stir in marshmallows until melted.
4. Add crispy rice cereal and stir.
5. Pour into a 13 x 9-inch greased pan. With a greasy spatula or finger, gently pat down to even out.
6. Sprinkle remaining sea salt on top. For extra Halloween flair, add black and orange sprinkles on top.
7. Once cool, cut into squares.

MOLLY McINTIRE

Dress-up is an American girl pastime, and Molly McIntire's trick-or-treating story and hula outfit are iconic in the American Girl canon. Hula costumes were historically common in the 1940s, but it's important to note that they could now be seen as cultural appropriation due to hula's deep Native Hawaiian significance. Molly tries hard to come up with a crackerjack costume that will be the envy of all the other apple bobbers. But Molly has an additional challenge given World War II restrictions: the costume must be made from readily available materials. Her craftiness is pure inspo—even future Historical Character Courtney Moore is inspired by Molly's creative costume!

Molly's influence carried over to the real world. Girls have been dressing up as AG dolls for decades, especially as Molly, one of the first three Historical Characters. Like her hula costume, it's easily made from clothes from the closet. Using just a few tricks, girls popped on round glasses, a Peter Pan collared blouse under an argyle sweater, and topped off braided pigtails with a blue beret and enjoyed the treat of looking like their favorite American Girl.

Cranberry Pumpkin Penny-Pincher Pancakes

KIT KITTREDGE,
Historical Character 1934

MAKES 4 SERVINGS/ SWEETS AND DESSERTS

Thanksgiving is a pivotal moment for Kit. While she and her friends Ruthie Smithens and Stirling Howard are donating a Thanksgiving basket to a soup kitchen, Kit spots her father waiting in the bread line. Realizing her family is in worse financial shape than she thought, she comes up with an inspired idea to reallocate the lumber intended for her treehouse to instead build an additional room onto their home so they can take in more boarders—and thereby keep the house and the family together.

Kit's mother has tricks to make a boardinghouse breakfast feel special, like placing a thin slice of peach on top of oatmeal to make it look fancy. During the Depression, cranberries and pumpkins were inexpensive ingredients. Combining the two and serving as mini pancakes, or let's say penny pancakes, turns a standard breakfast into a refined meal to fill up happy foodie friends.

INGREDIENTS

1 cup maple syrup

½ cup cranberries

3½ tablespoons unsalted butter, divided

1 cup all-purpose flour

1 tablespoon light brown sugar, lightly packed

1 teaspoon baking powder

¼ teaspoon salt

1¼ cups milk

1 teaspoon vanilla extract

¼ teaspoon ground cinnamon

¼ teaspoon nutmeg

1 egg

⅔ cup canned pumpkin puree

1 teaspoon powdered sugar

KIT KITTREDGE

Kit Kittredge lived during the difficulties of the Depression but tries to keep an attitude as cheery as her lavender cardigan and bouncy as her blonde bob. Introduced in 2000, the aspiring journalist was the seventh Historical Character and quickly became an icon and favorite for AG fans. Who could resist her floppy-eared basset hound Gracie or her inventive homemade soapbox scooter? If you were a Kit girl, you definitely admired her "short hair don't care" attitude. An aspiring reporter, when the financial crisis hits, she founds *The Hard Times News* newsletter, which she creates with her trusty typewriter—both accessories from her collection.

RECIPE STEPS

1. Preheat oven to 200°F.
2. Combine maple syrup and cranberries in a small saucepan. Heat on low, stirring regularly, until cranberries pop.
3. In a small microwave-safe bowl, heat 1½ tablespoons butter in the microwave for 30 seconds, or until melted.
4. In a large bowl, mix flour, brown sugar, baking powder, and salt until combined.
5. In a medium bowl, whisk melted butter, milk, vanilla extract, cinnamon, nutmeg, and egg.
6. Add the milk mixture and pumpkin puree to the large bowl with the flour mixture. Mix into a batter.
7. Coat a large nonstick skillet with cooking spray and bring to temperature over medium heat.
8. Ladle ¼ cup of the batter onto the skillet until it expands into a small circle. Add as many pancakes to the griddle as possible without touching.
9. Cook the pancakes for about 2 minutes, until the pancake tops bubble and the bottoms turn golden-brown. Flip each pancake with a spatula and cook another minute longer, until golden-brown.
10. Keep completed pancakes warm on a platter in oven while repeating steps 8 and 9 with the rest of the batter.
11. Sprinkle the pancakes with powdered sugar and top each serving with ½ tablespoon butter and the cranberry maple syrup.

Coffee Grind Brisket

NICKI HOFFMAN,
Historical Character 1999

**MAKES 8 SERVINGS/
MAIN MUNCHIES**

Brisket is a favorite dish served on Jewish holidays, such as Hanukkah, Passover, and Shabbat. Like the grinds and ollies that Nikki is trying to master on her skateboard, this brisket has a trick: using an espresso rub to bring out the rich, savory flavor of the meat.

INGREDIENTS

3 to 4 pounds brisket, fat cap trimmed to ½ inch

2 teaspoons Worcestershire sauce

1½ teaspoons salt

¾ tablespoon chili powder

¾ tablespoon cayenne powder

1 teaspoon cumin

1 teaspoon garlic powder

1 teaspoon black pepper

2 tablespoons light brown sugar, lightly packed

¼ teaspoon red pepper flakes

2 tablespoons extra-virgin olive oil

2 cloves garlic, minced

1 cup ketchup

½ cup honey

¼ cup balsamic vinegar

⅛ cup soy sauce

1 tablespoon chili garlic sauce

⅛ cup coffee, freshly brewed

RECIPE STEPS

1. The night before cooking and serving the brisket, rinse and then dry brisket with paper towels. Brush Worcestershire sauce on entire brisket.

2. Combine salt, chili powder, cayenne powder, cumin, garlic powder, black pepper, brown sugar, and red pepper flakes. Reserve half for use the next day. Spread the remaining spice rub over entire brisket.

3. Place brisket in a roasting pan, cover, and refrigerate overnight.

4. The next day, start by preheating oven to 250°F.

5. Remove brisket from the refrigerator and cover it with the remaining spice mix. Cover and place into oven for 3 to 4 hours (about 1 hour for every pound of brisket).

6. While brisket bakes, make the sauce. Heat the olive oil in a small saucepan over medium-low heat. Add garlic and sauté for about 1 minute until it turns lightly brown. Remove from heat. Whisk into saucepan the ketchup, honey, balsamic vinegar, soy sauce, chili garlic sauce, and coffee. Simmer the sauce on medium-low heat for 10 minutes, stirring regularly.

7. Once brisket reaches an internal temperature of 165°F, remove from oven. Pour off any fat from the bottom of the roasting pan, which can be reserved for another recipe. Pour three-quarters of the sauce over the brisket.

8. Increase oven temperature to 350°F. Return brisket to oven, uncovered, for 30 minutes or until the internal temperature of the brisket reaches 180°F. Remove from oven and let rest for 15 minutes.

9. Slice brisket into ½-inch strips, top with remaining sauce, and serve.

NICKI HOFFMAN

Nicki Hoffman is a Historical Character if you can believe it—a historical millennial! She grew up in the late '90s in Seattle, and like many proud millennials, she rocks chunky highlights, a backward cap, and platform sneakers. She's the total opposite of twin Isabel—Nicki is shy, organized, and quiet. Where Isabel leaps at the chance to dance to the Spice Girls or NSYNC on a stage in front of strangers, Nicki avoids the spotlight and pop music. Instead, she's a skater girl who listens to grunge. When Nicki starts writing lyrics, she sparks her dad's interest in music again, a passion he had put to the side while he dealt with his struggling coffee shop. Nicki and Isabel come together to concoct a plan to revitalize the shop during New Year's Eve and, in doing so, reignite his passion to perform.

Sugar Plum Fairy Punch

ISABELLE PALMER,
Girl of the Year 2014

**MAKES 1 DRINK/
COCKTAILS AND MOCKTAILS**

This holiday punch combines inspiration from Isabelle's Christmas pirouettes in *The Nutcracker* and her spring performance as a prancing sea fairy. Using the colors of her adorable pink and purple leotards and costumes, this sparkling punch will keep you on your toes and jeté your gathering to the stars.

INGREDIENTS

1½ ounces vodka
1 ounce plum liqueur
1 ounce pomegranate juice
¼ ounce grenadine
½ cup ginger ale
¼ ounce lemon juice (optional)
Edible glitter, for garnish

RECIPE STEPS

1. Pour all the ingredients into a tall glass over ice. Stir.
2. Take a sip. If it's too sweet, add some lemon juice for balance.
3. Sprinkle some edible glitter on top for added dazzle.

The Isabelle Palmer Mocktail

ISABELLE PALMER,
Girl of the Year 2014

**MAKES 12 DRINKS/
COCKTAILS AND MOCKTAILS**

In *The Nutcracker*, Isabelle is cast as one of Mother Ginger's children, getting the spotlight role of the Gingerbread Girl. Tart, sweet, and bubbly, ginger elevates this lemonade-based beverage to offer all you want for Christmas in one glass.

INGREDIENTS

1 cup lemon juice, freshly squeezed (about 4 to 6 lemons)

½ to ¾ cup granulated sugar (adjust to taste)

1 cup pomegranate juice

4 cups cold water

½ cup ginger ale

Lemon slice, for garnish

Pomegranate arils, for garnish

Mint leaf, for garnish

RECIPE STEPS

1. To make the lemonade base, squeeze lemon juice into a pitcher and add sugar, starting with ½ cup. Stir until sugar is dissolved.

2. Add pomegranate juice and stir.

3. Add water to the pitcher and stir completely. Taste, and if it's not sweet enough, stir in more sugar, 1 tablespoon at a time.

4. Refrigerate pomegranate lemonade mixture for at least 1 hour, until chilled.

5. To serve, pour ½ cup of the mixture into a tall glass filled with ice. Top with ½ cup ginger ale.

6. Garnish with a lemon slice, a few pomegranate arils, and a mint leaf, if desired.

ISABELLE PALMER

Girl of the Year 2014 Isabelle Palmer is finally invited to attend exclusive Anna Hart School of the Arts where big sis Jade is the top dancer and student. Self-conscious in her sister's shadow, Isabelle lacks self-confidence, but with her electric pink hair extensions, we all know she's bound to blossom. When she dances "The Waltz of the Flowers" in a costume she created, the dance director takes notice—she's cast in *The Nutcracker* and tapped to design the costumes (which we were invited to take part in with her sewing studio and human-size fashion sketchbook). When New York Ballet ballerina Jackie Sanchez takes her under her wing, Isabelle realizes she's got her own unique pirouette on life.

Happy Birthday

CHAPTER 7

Birthday Bliss

American Girl and birthdays go together like cake and ice cream, and AG dolls were at the top of the gift wish list. Many of us AG fans remember unwrapping our birthday presents to find our dream dolls underneath, sparking a lifelong love for the brand. American Girl–themed birthday parties were always exciting because, just like Samantha Parkington's fancy party, guests would bring their dolls and serve them tiny slices of cake. Some girls celebrated their birthdays at the American Girl Café, with everyone's doll getting her own seat at the table and all the attendees leaving with goody bags full of adorable doll T-shirts and accessories. The experience is so incredible, the café is attracting AG adults who relish the novelty of putting on a crown and celebrating our adulthood with our childhood dolls. These recipes are a reminder that you may be getting older, but it's never too late to celebrate your inner child.

Birthday Bagel Dogs

LINDSEY BERGMAN,
Girl of the Year 2001

**MAKES 12 BAGEL DOGS/
APPETIZERS AND SNACKS**

Back in 2001, Lindsey brought a new kind of inclusiveness to American Girl dolls: diversity of faith. The first Girl of the Year is Jewish, and her family is focused on brother Ethan's upcoming bar mitzvah—a birthday celebration and coming-of-age in the Jewish tradition. Lindsey, on the other hand, is occupied with "improving" the lives of her neighbors—without consulting them first. But when her dog, Mr. Tiny, is lost, her puppy love is so strong, the neighborhood puts their annoyance with her aside and rallies to help find her beloved dachshund. Later, when her brother worries he'll blow it at his bar mitzvah, he turns to her for comfort, and Lindsey realizes giving help to someone who asks for it is the best mitzvah there is.

Bagel dogs are the perfect pop-in-your-mouth pleasers for a birthday party. Your guests will be begging for more!

INGREDIENTS

- 1 teaspoon dehydrated onion
- 1 teaspoon sesame seeds
- 1 teaspoon poppy seeds
- ¼ teaspoon garlic powder
- ¼ teaspoon plus ½ teaspoon kosher salt, divided
- ¾ cup plus 1 tablespoon lukewarm water, divided
- ¾ teaspoon active dry yeast
- 2 cups all-purpose flour
- ¼ tablespoon brown sugar, lightly packed
- 1 teaspoon extra-virgin olive oil, for greasing
- 12 cocktail franks
- ¼ cup honey
- 1 egg
- 1 tablespoon water
- ¼ teaspoon sugar

LINDSEY BERGMAN

One year into the new millennium, American Girl launched their very first Girl of the Year with the unstoppable Lindsey Bergman. Well intentioned, she does "good deeds" no one is asking for, including protecting pets from wearing costumes in a parade, beautifying the community by covering trash cans with stickers, and making romantic connections for her teachers, one of whom is engaged to someone else (whoops). Things take a turn when Uncle Bernie loses Lindsey's dachshund Mr. Tiny. Former foe Josh finds her runaway pooch, surprising her with his kindness and a new perspective.

RECIPE STEPS

1. To make everything bagel spice, toss dehydrated onion, sesame seeds, poppy seeds, garlic powder, and ¼ teaspoon salt in a small bowl. Set aside.

2. Whisk ¾ cup lukewarm water and yeast in a medium-sized mixing bowl. Let stand for 10 minutes.

3. Add flour, brown sugar, and ½ teaspoon salt to the yeast and water mixture. Mix (with a mixer or wooden spoon) until combined into a dough.

4. Transfer the dough to a lightly floured surface. Knead by hand for 7 minutes. If the dough remains sticky, add a teaspoon of flour while kneading.

5. Grease a large bowl with olive oil. Transfer the dough to the greased bowl, cover, and let rise for an hour.

6. Preheat oven to 425°F.

7. Once risen, divide the dough into twelve 1-inch balls of dough. Roll each ball into a 6-inch "rope," about the thickness of a pencil.

8. In a spiral shape, wrap each rope around a cocktail frank. Spear a toothpick through the frank and each end of the dough rope, to keep the dough-rolled frank intact. Place each dough-rolled frank on a greased baking sheet.

9. Mix honey into a large pot of water. Bring to a boil. Working in batches, boil 4 to 6 dough-rolled franks at a time for 60 seconds, turning over once while boiling if needed. Return franks to the baking sheet after boiling.

10. Whisk egg with 1 tablespoon water and ¼ teaspoon sugar in a small bowl. Using a pastry brush, brush the surface of each of the dough-wrapped franks with the egg wash. Sprinkle each with everything bagel spice from Step 1.

11. Bake the bagel dogs for 20 minutes until golden-brown, turning the pan around halfway through to bake evenly.

12. Transfer to a wire rack to cool. Serve with favorite condiments.

Palomino Fancy Bow Tie Pasta

LILA MONETTI,
Girl of the Year 2024

MAKES 8 SERVINGS/ MAIN MUNCHIES

Lila is the first American Girl of Italian descent. And, if there's one thing Italians are known for, it's the tradition of enjoying a delicious pasta dish. This bow tie pasta recipe is a nod to Lila's roots, and the caramelized onions and farfalle recognize her stylish flair with horse hairstyles. This satisfying dish is great for a large birthday gathering to feed your friends and family and can make the occasion feel extra fancy.

INGREDIENTS

3 medium sweet yellow onions, thinly sliced

2 shallots, thinly sliced

½ teaspoon fresh rosemary needles, chopped

3 tablespoons balsamic glaze

¼ cup salt, divided

1½ teaspoons black pepper, divided

½ cup oil from sun-dried tomato jar

1 bulb garlic

2 tablespoons extra-virgin olive oil, divided

2 tablespoons pine nuts

2 links Italian sausage (about ¼ pound)

½ cup white wine

1 pound bow tie pasta

½ teaspoon red pepper flakes, crushed

¼ cup sun-dried tomato pesto

1 16-ounce jar sun-dried tomatoes, chopped

½ teaspoon sugar

1 cup thinly sliced fresh basil

¼ cup Parmesan cheese, grated

RECIPE STEPS

1. Preheat oven to 350°F.

2. In a large (13 x 9-inch) baking dish, toss onions and shallots with rosemary, balsamic glaze, 1 teaspoon each salt and black pepper, and oil from the sun-dried tomato jar.

3. Cover and roast for 15 minutes.

4. While onions roast, chop the top off of the bulb of garlic, exposing the tops of the garlic cloves. Form a small bowl out of aluminum foil and place the bulb in the foil. Top the exposed cloves of garlic with 1 tablespoon olive oil and a pinch of salt and pepper. Fold up the sides of foil and twist to seal the bulb in the foil.

5. After onions have roasted for 15 minutes, uncover, stir, cover, and roast for another 60 minutes.

6. Place the foil-wrapped garlic bulb in oven and roast for 60 minutes.

7. While onions and garlic bulb roast, heat a medium skillet over medium heat. Once up to temperature, add pine nuts to the pan and toast for 1 minute, stirring often. Remove pine nuts and set aside.

8. In the same skillet, over medium heat, add 1 tablespoon olive oil. Remove Italian sausage links from their casings and add to the skillet. Using a spatula or wooden spoon, break sausage into small pieces. Stirring often, cook for 4 to 5 minutes, until browned. Remove sausage to a plate and set aside.

9. Still in the same skillet over medium heat, deglaze the skillet with white wine. Use a wooden spoon to remove the sausage bits from the bottom of the skillet. Pour the deglaze and sausage bits into a medium heatproof bowl. Set aside.

10. Fill a large saucepan with water. Add remaining salt. Bring to a boil. Cook pasta per the instructions. Reserve ¼ cup pasta water before draining.

11. Mix reserved pasta water, red pepper flakes, sun-dried tomato pesto, sun-dried tomatoes, and sugar into the bowl with the white wine deglaze.

12. After the onion mixture and garlic bulb are done roasting, remove from oven. Remove garlic from the foil bowl and, once cool, squeeze the bulb to release each clove into the pasta mixture.

13. Gently fold pasta and deglaze mixture into the roasted onion mixture.

14. Spoon into bowls, top with pine nuts, basil, and grated Parmesan, and dig in!

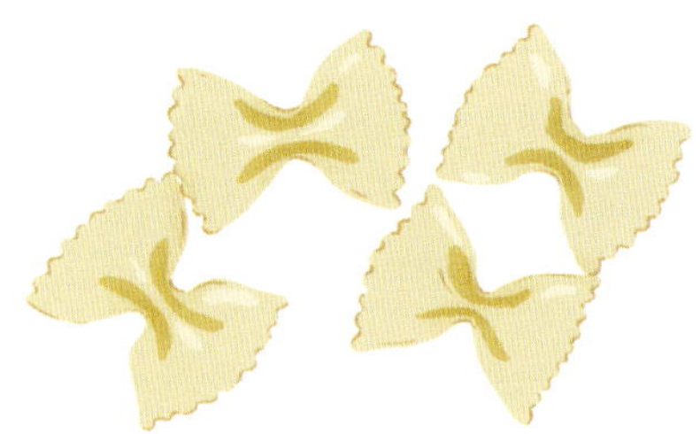

LILA MONETTI

Girl of the Year Lila Monetti flips when she's invited to join the Xcel gymnastics team and is all in. She's worried if she attends horse camp with her brother, she'll fall behind in gymnastics. But when Coach McKenna (yes, *that* McKenna, Girl of the Year 2012, now a college student!) says horseback riding will help her improve her balance, she agrees to go, even though that means she's now the new girl in *two* social groups. That outsider feeling draws her to a Palomino named Hollyhock, the newest horse at Honeycrisp Hill. Hollyhock hasn't acclimated to the other horses yet and is kept in a separate paddock. Lila learns Hollyhock may have to be sold if she can't be trained.

Connecting with Hollyhock is the *mane* priority for Lila, who gains the mare's trust by grooming her. Lila gives her a mane-over, clipping in colorful extensions, elegant braids, and beautiful bows. Lila then trains Mighty Mae, the camp corgi, to run alongside Hollyhock on their rides, getting the horse used to the other animals so that she doesn't get spooked. Lila makes sure Hollyhock has a forever home at Honeycrisp Hill.

Queen Bee's Knees Martini

SONALI MATTHEWS,
Friend of Girl of the Year 2009

**MAKES 1 DRINK/
COCKTAILS AND MOCKTAILS**

Sonali Matthews becomes a friend of Girl of the Year 2009 Chrissa Maxwell. At first, Sonali is a member of the popular Queen Bees. But when the teasing goes too far, Sonali stands strong beside Chrissa. She bravely tells the truth and brings the Queen Bees to their knees.

The Bee's Knees cocktail is a favorite for adult patrons of the American Girl Café (and, as previously mentioned, a popular destination for adult AG fans to celebrate their birthday!). This recipe originated during Prohibition when bootleggers were stirring up gin in their bathtubs. It wasn't the tastiest of beverages, and the Bee's Knees recipe was made to mask the flavor with healthy heaps of lemon and honey. This cocktail is the bee's knees (the "best" in jazz speak), a perfect concoction to celebrate a birthday with your friends.

INGREDIENTS

Lavender honey syrup

½ cup water

½ cup honey

2 teaspoons dried lavender blossoms or 1 large sprig of fresh lavender

Cocktail or mocktail

1 ounce lavender honey syrup

¾ ounce lemon juice, freshly squeezed

2 ounces dry gin, for cocktail

2 ounces club soda, for mocktail

1 or 2 dashes lavender bitters (optional)

Lavender sprig, for garnish

Lemon twist, for garnish

RECIPE STEPS

To make the lavender honey syrup:

1. In a small saucepan over medium heat, heat water, honey, and lavender. Stir lightly until honey dissolves.

2. Remove from heat and strain out blossoms. Set aside to cool.

3. There will be more than needed, so store the leftover in the refrigerator for up to two weeks. The syrup can be used in other cocktails and recipes.

To make the cocktail or mocktail:

1. When it's time to prepare the cocktail, pour lavender honey syrup, lemon juice, and gin into a shaker filled with ice. For the mocktail, substitute club soda for gin.

2. Give a good shake, then strain into a chilled martini or coupe glass.

3. Add a dash or two of lavender bitters, if desired. Garnish with a lavender sprig or a lemon twist. Cheers to friendship and forgiveness!

SONALI MATTHEWS

In 2009, Sonali Matthews truly "broke the mold" as the first Indian American Girl. She ushered in a couple of other firsts: Sonali and Gwen Thompson were the first best friend dolls for a Girl of the Year and marks the first time a doll was given a set of friend dolls rather than just one.

Daytona Dreamsicle Shake

MARYELLEN LARKIN,
Historical Character 1954

**MAKES 1 DRINK/
COCKTAILS AND MOCKTAILS**

It's not a birthday without ice cream! Taste 1950s childhood with this creamsicle drink, perfect for sipping with Maryellen at the Seaside Diner. Add a little whipped cream vodka for a more grown-up version.

INGREDIENTS

⅛ cup heavy cream

1 ounce whipped cream vodka (optional)

1 cup orange sherbet

1 cup vanilla ice cream

Whipped cream, for garnish

Sprinkles, for garnish

RECIPE STEPS

1. In a blender, pour heavy cream and whipped cream vodka, if desired.

2. Add orange sherbet and vanilla ice cream.

3. Blend until smooth. If too thick, add more heavy cream.

4. Pour into a parfait glass. Top with whipped cream and sprinkles. Pop in a straw and sip!

MARYELLEN LARKIN

Maryellen Larkin is vibrant and brimming with new ideas. She is a Historical Character representing the 1950s, with ambitions as high as her ponytail and a desire to stand out with flair as wide as her poodle skirt. When she transforms her birthday party into a March of Dimes fundraiser, her starry dreams come true. Her encouragement to families to get the polio vaccine gets recognition from Daytona's mayor, elevating Maryellen to local celebrity status.

Would Maryellen grow up to defy the era's societal limitations on women and become a rocket scientist for NASA? Or did she take on the hard job of motherhood and raise a family? Or did she do both? The great thing about playing with dolls is that the decision is entirely up to you.

Petticoats and Pink Lemonade Petit Fours

SAMANTHA PARKINGTON,
Historical Character 1904

MAKES 6–7 DOZEN SERVINGS/ SWEETS AND DESSERTS

As the American Girl hostess with the most-ess, Samantha knows that festive décor and fancy food help make an event a success. For her tenth birthday party, Samantha asks Mrs. Hawkins to make her tiny cakes, one for each year of her life. The cook is a bit taken aback, as petit fours take more effort than a standard cake. Indeed, it is a task. But in the end, you'll have a charming display of tiny cakes that look like presents!

INGREDIENTS

Lemon curd

1 cup granulated sugar

1 tablespoon lemon zest

6 egg whites

½ cup lemon juice, freshly squeezed (about 2 lemons)

⅛ teaspoon salt

½ cup unsalted butter, cut into 8 pats

Cake

3¼ cups cake flour

1 teaspoon baking powder

½ teaspoon salt

1½ cups unsalted butter, room temperature

1 8-ounce package cream cheese, room temperature

3 cups granulated sugar

1 teaspoon vanilla extract

1 cup milk

6 eggs, room temperature

2 cups lemon curd

16 ounces raspberry or strawberry preserves

Buttercream frosting (see recipe on page 65)

Pink food coloring

Glaze

8 cups powdered sugar, sifted

½ cup water

½ cup light corn syrup

1 teaspoon vanilla extract

½ teaspoon lemon extract (optional)

Food coloring (optional)

Sprinkles

RECIPE STEPS

To make the lemon curd:

1. Place granulated sugar and lemon zest in a food processor. Pulse until zest is thoroughly minced.

2. In a saucepan, combine egg whites, lemon juice, and salt. Whisk.

3. Whisk in the sugar-zest mixture until mixed.

4. Move saucepan to the stove, on low heat, whisking while it thickens. When it starts to bubble and an inserted spoon has a light coating, it's ready.

5. Remove from heat. Add butter, mixing completely.

6. Transfer to a container and place plastic wrap across the top, touching the top of the curd to prevent a skin from forming.

7. Chill in the refrigerator for an hour before using. Or, if made in advance, the curd can be refrigerated for ten days and frozen for three months.

To make the cake:

1. Preheat oven to 325°F.

2. Use shortening to grease two 11 x 17-inch baking sheets with edges, placing parchment papers on the bottom as well.

3. Sift cake flour, baking powder, and salt into a medium-size bowl. Set aside.

4. Using an electric or stand mixer, beat butter in a large bowl until smooth.

5. Add cream cheese and mix until blended completely.

6. Slowly add sugar, mixing until light and fluffy.

7. Add in vanilla extract and milk.

8. Drop in eggs one at a time, beating at low speed before adding the next.

9. Once totally combined, slowly mix in the flour mixture on a low speed.

10. Pour the batter into the two baking sheets, dividing equally. Spread evenly.

11. Bake for 35 to 40 minutes. Remove from oven when top springs back when touched and a toothpick is inserted and comes out clean.

12. Once cool, wrap tightly and put in the freezer until ready to move on to the next step, for at least an hour.

13. Removing cakes from the freezer, spread a thin layer of lemon curd on one cake. Spread a thin layer of preserves on the other. (If filling is thick, it will spill out once cut.)

14. Use the parchment paper to lift the cake with the preserves out of the pan. Flip face down onto the other cake so that it's completely lined up.

15. Rewrap and place cake in the freezer for at least 45 minutes (however, if wrapped tightly, cakes can stay in the freezer for weeks).

16. Make the buttercream frosting. Stir in pink food coloring so that color is even.

17. Remove the cake from the freezer and ice the cake. Return to the freezer for at least an hour (it's easier to cut a frozen cake).

18. Removing cake from the freezer, use the parchment paper to lift cake out of pan and place onto a large cutting board.

19. Trim the edges of the frozen cake. Cut into 1½-inch squares. (Don't go as small as 1 inch; they need to be wide enough to sit on the wire racks.) Return to the freezer.

To make the glaze:

1. Set a pot of water on the stove on medium heat.

2. In a large heatproof bowl, mix powdered sugar, water, corn syrup, vanilla extract, and, if desired, lemon extract.

3. Place the bowl over the simmering water (the bowl should be above, but not touching, the water inside the pot) and continue to stir until smooth.

4. If a color is desired, stir in food coloring.

To ice the petit fours:

1. Set up wire cooling racks over some kind of protected surface to collect drips, such as wax paper, silicone mat, or a baking sheet.

2. One at a time, slide a large serving fork under one of the tiny, layered cakes. Hold the cake over the bowl with the glaze. Use a spoon to pour the glaze over the cake, letting the glaze drip down the sides. Allow excess to drip back into the bowl.

3. Slide the cake onto the wire cooling rack.

4. If there is too much filling and the top layer is sliding, insert a toothpick to hold it into place.

5. Repeat until all the cakes are iced and cooling. Keep the glaze warm, returning it to the simmering water if you've removed it to be closer to your wire racks. Be advised, these do make a *lot* of little cakes. You may want to make a smaller quantity and freeze the rest of the cake for another time.

6. If using sprinkles to decorate, add as soon as you set the cakes on cooling rack, before glaze sets.

7. Otherwise, wait for glaze to set before decorating, about an hour. You can use writing icing to decorate the cakes to look like gifts with ribbons and, of course, add a bow on top for an authentic Samantha finish!

SAMANTHA PARKINGTON

With her adventurous spirit, gorgeous style, and rich historical storyline, Samantha Parkington has long been a fan favorite, inviting readers to imagine what her life was like at the turn of the twentieth century. One of the original three American Girl dolls released in 1986, Edwardian-era Samantha might have complained about her itchy long underwear, but the rest of her wardrobe was divine: a burgundy and ivory checked dress, a birthday party pink taffeta pinstriped frock, and a blue bicycle outfit with pantaloons. If you were a Samantha girl, it's likely you had quite the hair accessory collection—the doll's ability to rock a bow was total goals—and you probably tried to convince your parents to match her décor so you, too, could have a brass bed with a precious white ruffled and ribboned bedspread.

Birthday Cake Martini

SUMMER McKINNY,
Girl of the Year 2025

MAKES 1 DRINK/
COCKTAILS AND MOCKTAILS

Dressing in pastel rainbow colors, Summer's fashion resembles sprinkles on a birthday cake. And with Summer and her can-do attitude, as soon as you blow out the candles on your birthday cake and make a wish, Summer will make it happen!

For birthdays of girls twenty-one and older, a great year starts with birthday cake sips that are as white and fluffy as Summer's dog, Crescent.

INGREDIENTS

½ tablespoon colorful sprinkles
1 teaspoon simple syrup
2 ounces whipped cream vodka
2 ounces white chocolate liqueur
1 ounce amaretto
2 ounces half-and-half

RECIPE STEPS

1. Pour the sprinkles on a small, flat plate. Moisten the rim of a martini glass with simple syrup, then roll the rim of the glass on the outside across the sprinkled plate.
2. Pour whipped cream vodka, white chocolate liqueur, amaretto, and half-and-half into a cocktail shaker full of ice.
3. Shake for 30 seconds.
4. Strain into the sprinkle-rimmed martini glass. Make a wish!

SUMMER MCKINNY

The Girl of the Year 2025 is a dog lover, dog walker, and baker! Summer McKinny has never met an idea she didn't like, launching into business ideas almost the second the light bulb goes on. With her sunny disposition, she even trains a visiting cat and her rambunctious dog—who fight like, well, cats and dogs—to get along.

CHAPTER 8

You Can Sip with Us

While the generations before us may have felt that being grown up meant getting rid of childhood playthings, we now realize that when something makes us happy, keep it around! While others might collect Rubik's Cubes, comic books, or figures from a galaxy far, far away, we have a deeper connection with our American Girl dolls. They connect us to who we were as kids and help us understand how we became the people we are today. The following cocktail recipes, inspired by the Historical Characters, are an embrace of our adulthood present and our childhood memories that shaped us.

Sipping these sophisticated beverages with your fellow AG-fan friends, you're transported back through time. You're gleefully flooded with a montage of memories and moments you shared with your doll as a kid, and then brought forward into the now with the self-satisfaction that you got through it, you made it, you're on the other side! Sitting with your friends and reminiscing about your shared doll experiences, you are overcome with joy and relief that even though each girlhood is unique, there is a sacred understanding held among all of you.

Starting there, let's raise a glass to our friends, who were our emotional rocks through the tough tween years, with cocktail and mocktail recipes inspired by the AG dolls and characters that bonded us. Cheers!

Felici-Tea

FELICITY MERRIMAN,
Historical Character 1775

MAKES 1 DRINK/
COCKTAILS AND MOCKTAILS

Felicity's acceptance into polite society is dependent on her education, including learning how to do needlework, dance elegantly, and absolutely, most importantly, serve tea. When her father protests the tea tax, astute Felicity demonstrates she supports her father and self-government when she turns over her cup of controversy in her weekly lessons with Miss Manderly and gracefully states to the host, "Thank you, I shall take no tea."

Celebrate Felicity with a cocktail that's as strong as her spirit and as bold and well balanced as Mr. Merriman's actions. Whether celebrating upending a monarchy or spilling the tea with friends, it's revolutionary!

In 1964, the US Congress declared bourbon "America's official native spirit." Although that innovation is credited to Kentucky, Kentucky was still Virginia in 1776. Instrumental in creating a new government and a new hooch, Virginians were brimming with the spirit of '76.

INGREDIENTS

Mint simple syrup

½ cup water

½ cup sugar

¼ cup mint leaves

Cocktail or mocktail

2 ounces chilled black tea

½ ounce lemon juice, freshly squeezed

2 ounces mint simple syrup

1½ ounces bourbon, for cocktail

Mint sprig, for garnish and extra flavor

Lemon wheel, for garnish*

RECIPE STEPS

To make the mint simple syrup:

1. In a small saucepan over high heat, bring water and sugar to a boil.

2. Once sugar is dissolved, remove from heat.

3. Add mint and steep for 30 minutes, while it cools.

4. Strain out mint leaves.

5. Set aside or put in the refrigerator until you're ready to use. The syrup can be made days in advance and will keep for a month or longer in the refrigerator if kept in a clean, airtight container. (Once it turns cloudy, toss it.)

To make the cocktail or mocktail:

1. Into a cocktail shaker with ice, pour black tea, lemon juice, mint simple syrup, and bourbon. For the mocktail, leave out bourbon.

2. Shake for 30 seconds.

3. Pour into a rocks glass with ice. The drink should have a nice froth.

4. Tear mint leaves on sprig to open flavor and sprinkle on top. Garnish with lemon wheel.

*To make a lemon wheel garnish, cut lemon into ⅛-inch to ¼-inch slices. On one slice, cut from center to rind. Place the opening onto the rim of glass.

FELICITY MERRIMAN

More than apple butter is churning in Williamsburg, Virginia, in 1774—rebellion is in the air! At the center is American Girl's fourth Historical Character and first horse girl, Felicity Merriman, who takes down abusive animal owners and the monarchy with bold spunk. Girls who connected with this red-headed iconic Historical Character tended to be equally feisty, carving out their own path and were quick to act against unjust behavior.

Felicity defies her parents and sneaks out of the house in the middle of the night to break and ride mean neighbor Jiggy Nye's horse Penny. She eventually sets Penny free (a scene many recreated with their own Penny play horse and Felicity's forest-green riding habit, complete with tri-corner hat!). Later, Felicity slips out in the middle of the night again to stop the British from stealing gunpowder, and she hides her friend Ben in the woods when he runs away to join the Patriot army. Real-life rule followers may find her actions a bit hard to swallow, but Felicity is just a normal colonial girl, figuring out her boundaries at a time when the rules are unclear: Should a girl be loyal to the royals, or does perfidiousness show patriotism?

Mezcal Mule

JOSEFINA MONTOYA,
Historical Character 1824

MAKES 1 DRINK/
COCKTAILS AND MOCKTAILS

This sparkly beverage honors the reliable animals that restore happiness to Josefina in the form of Tia Dolores, her mother's sister from Mexico, whose hair has a touch of ginger. Just as mules were essential to the trading caravans that supported Josefina's Santa Fe community, mezcal is a uniquely Mexican alcohol that supports the local economies that produce it.

INGREDIENTS

¼ teaspoon candied ginger, diced
½ ounce mezcal, for cocktail
1½ ounces tequila, for cocktail
½ to 1 ounce fresh lime juice
4 ounces ginger beer
1 ounce agave syrup, for mocktail
Lime slice, for garnish
Mint leaves, for garnish

RECIPE STEPS

1. To brighten this drink, start by putting candied ginger in the bottom of a copper mug.

2. Pour in mezcal, tequila, ½ ounce lime juice, and ginger beer. For the mocktail, leave out mezcal and tequila, use 1 ounce lime juice, and add agave syrup. Add ice.

3. Garnish with lime slice and mint leaves.

JOSEFINA MONTOYA

Mules may not be as high profile as goats in Josefina Montoya's story, but the pack animals move Josefina's story forward. Josefina's abuelito, the father of her recently deceased Mamá, makes an annual trading trek to Mexico City with a massive caravan that includes more than a hundred mules to pull wagons loaded with goods to sell and trade.

After Josefina befriends Patrick, a scout and Americano, Papá trusts him to trade his mules for much-needed silver. When Patrick disappears, Papá assumes the worst and plans to leave at daybreak to retrieve his mules from the Americanos, which will scorch both his and Patrick's reputations. But when the moonlight illuminates a secret message Patrick left her, Josefina sneaks out in the middle of the night to confirm Patrick didn't break his promise. After a night of adventure, Josefina saves the day, stopping Papá from doing something he'd regret. That's cause for celebration!

Prairie Punch

KIRSTEN LARSON,
Historical Character 1854

MAKES 1 DRINK/
COCKTAILS AND MOCKTAILS

In honor of Kirsten's strength, sweetness, and survival skills, Prairie Punch has a hearty base but presents soft with a tender stone fruit.

INGREDIENTS

1½ ounces Scotch
½ ounce peach liqueur
1 tablespoon lemon juice
1 tablespoon simple syrup
¼ cup coconut water
¼ cup club soda
Mint sprig, for garnish
Peach slice, for garnish

RECIPE STEPS

1. In a cocktail shaker filled with ice, combine Scotch, peach liqueur, lemon juice, simple syrup, and coconut water. Shake.
2. Strain into a tall glass filled with ice. Top with club soda.
3. Garnish with mint sprig and peach slice.

KIRSTEN LARSON

Living on a homestead on a Minnesota prairie, Kirsten Larson is brave in the face of nature's worst, facing a blizzard, twister, and angry mamma bear. The Larsons worked hard, and when it came time to relax, well, that still involved hard work. Whether that was a barn raising, a sewing circle, or trading goods during the Independence Day parade, even fun, festive events were filled with work. Although Kirsten is hard at work, helping the family out around the farm, she finds ways to express her creativity and have fun in ways that are meaningful to her, like playing dolls with her cousins, learning to make a quilt, gathering with friends, and playing with her cat, Missy, and her kittens.

Ice Cream Dreams

ADDY WALKER,
Historical Character 1864

MAKES 5 DRINKS/
COCKTAILS AND MOCKTAILS

One of Addy's favorite treats is ice cream—something she tasted for the first time in Philadelphia at a church social. When her poppa finds a broken ice cream freezer, he wants to fix it up for Addy's birthday. But first, she needs to decide when her birthday will be! Like most formerly enslaved people, Addy didn't know the exact day she was born. But when the right day came, Addy knew it—April 9, the day in 1865 that the Civil War came to an end. The whole city of Philadelphia broke out in joyful celebration in the middle of the night, and Addy's family created a beautiful party just for her, complete with ice cream from the fixed freezer, cherry pie, and ginger pop. Things are far from easy in Philadelphia for Addy and her loved ones, but that day, Addy cherished happy moments with her family, yummy food, and laughter.

This sweet cocktail, a version of the Pink Squirrel cocktail, is a nod to Addy's favorite treat and great for a celebratory day, to remind us of the things that bring us joy.

INGREDIENTS

1 ounce white crème de cacao

1 ounce crème de almond or crème de noyaux (alternatively, you can use 1 ounce amaretto and add a dash of grenadine or red food coloring—for that pink effect)

2 scoops vanilla ice cream

Whipped cream, for garnish

Maraschino cherries, for garnish

RECIPE STEPS

1. Pour all ingredients into a blender and blend until smooth.
2. Pour into chilled coupe or cocktail glasses.
3. Add whipped cream on top and a cherry for extra joy!

ADDY WALKER

When Poppa suggested that maybe Sarah could help Addy pick a day for her birthday, Addy couldn't wait to have Sarah over to play. Addy prepared an indoor picnic just for the two of them. She spread out an old blanket and set out two small plates, two cups, and two spoons. Momma said they could have cornbread and milk for a treat. When Sarah arrived, Addy excitedly told Sarah that she could help pick her birthday! Sarah could think of many days that would be fun, but she wanted a day that meant the most to Addy. Like the true and selfless friend that she is, Sarah said, "I think you should pick it all by yourself."

Get the Vote Float

SAMANTHA PARKINGTON,
Historical Character 1904

As much as Grandmary is trying to mold Samantha Parkington into a proper young lady who believes the old ways are the best ways, Samantha is a girl under the influence of the fabulous Aunt Cornelia, a rebel role model rallying for equal rights. While Grandmary is firm in her thoughts about a lady's proper place, Aunt Cornelia speaks at protests with banners that read "WOMEN FIGHT FOR YOUR RIGHT TO VOTE." She's not afraid to speak up for women's right to equal pay and equal rights to participate in democracy. Eventually, after hearing Cornelia give one of her speeches, Grandmary softens to the cause.

This cocktail is a twist on the Suffragette cocktail that was invented in Minneapolis during this time, celebrating women like Aunt Cornelia for making a difference.

INGREDIENTS

1 ounce sloe gin
1 ounce dry vermouth
1 ounce sweet vermouth
2 dashes orange bitters
½ ounce limoncello, for float
Lemon twist, for garnish

RECIPE STEPS

1. In a mixing glass, combine the sloe gin, dry vermouth, sweet vermouth, and orange bitters.
2. Add ice and stir well until chilled.
3. Strain into a chilled cocktail glass.
4. To add the float, measure out ½ ounce limoncello. Hold a chilled spoon just above the surface of the cocktail, convex side up. Slowly pour limoncello over the back of the spoon so that it floats on top of the drink.
5. Garnish with a lemon twist.

SAMANTHA PARKINGTON

Although Samantha Parkington is initially jealous of the attention her beloved uncle Gard gives Cornelia, she soon sees what a fun person Cornelia is. She goes sledding and laughs when she falls in the snow, and she helps Samantha build a gingerbread house when no one else has the time. She is ultimately delighted when Uncle Gard proposes to Cornelia on Christmas Day!

Sparkling Victory Garden Cocktail

MOLLY McINTIRE,
Historical Character 1944

MAKES 1 DRINK/
COCKTAILS AND MOCKTAILS

Molly is a sparkler and has one of American Girl's most patriotic storylines. The book opens with Mrs. Gilford's Victory Garden, planted so she doesn't buy canned foods because tin is needed for the war effort. Molly's physician father is assigned to a medical unit in England, and her mother is often gone, volunteering with the Red Cross. War rationing means sugar is limited, no rubber for boots, and no new material for clothes or Halloween costumes.

But there's one recycled costume Molly yearns to wear—the colorful leotard and silver star crown that goes to the soloist in the "Hurray for the U.S.A.!" dance program. Trying to look the part, Molly bumps around without her glasses and endures weeks of hair experiments to get curls (sister Jill is a hair hero, saving Molly from a disastrous home perm). Perseverance pays off. Molly is named Miss Victory and shines in her red, white, and blue costume. To girls who nabbed this coveted wardrobe item before it was retired, cheers to you!

INGREDIENTS

1 ounce vodka
¾ ounce elderflower liqueur
1 ounce pineapple juice
¾ ounce lemon juice, freshly squeezed
½ ounce simple syrup
4 ounces Prosecco or Champagne
Sprig of rosemary, for garnish

RECIPE STEPS

1. Pour vodka, elderflower liqueur, pineapple juice, lemon juice, and simple syrup into a cocktail shaker and shake for 30 seconds.

2. Strain into a tall glass over ice.

3. Top with Prosecco or Champagne.

4. Finish with a sprig of rosemary.

MOLLY McINTIRE

Bespectacled and braided, Molly McIntire is one of the most recognizable American Girl dolls. While she goes trick-or-treating, attends summer camps, and participates in dance recitals, her childhood is also marked with hardships, with her father away at war, her mother suddenly away at work, and repercussions of the war played out at home, like air raid drills at school. Despite this, she keeps her spirits high. Except when she's faced with a dish of turnips!

Bridal Blusher

KAYA'ATON'MY,
Historical Character 1764

**MAKES 2 DRINKS/
COCKTAILS AND MOCKTAILS**

The next time romance has you as stressed as Kaya's older sister Brown Deer, when a potential in-law moved in to make sure Brown Deer was marriage-worthy, try this mellowing cocktail that has skullcap, a flowering plant in the mint family used to ease anxiety and stress. It's grown in the Pacific Northwest, as are the wild huckleberries in Kaya's trading feast accessory set. Pairing the native fruit with rosemary creates an unexpected flavor union.

INGREDIENTS

Rosemary simple syrup

⅓ cup water

⅓ cup sugar

5 sprigs rosemary, divided, 2 sprigs reserved for garnish

Mocktail

⅓ cup huckleberries (if not available, substitute blueberries), plus 4 to 6 more for garnish

1 cup sparkling water

2 tablespoons rosemary simple syrup

1½ ounces lime juice, freshly squeezed

½ tablespoon maple syrup

1 dropper of skullcap tincture

RECIPE STEPS

To make the rosemary simple syrup:

1. In a small saucepan over high heat, bring water, sugar, and 2 sprigs of rosemary to a boil.
2. Once sugar is dissolved, remove from heat.
3. Steep rosemary for 30 minutes, while it cools.
4. Strain out sprigs.
5. Set aside or put in the refrigerator until you're ready to use. The syrup can be made days in advance and will keep for a month or longer in the refrigerator if kept in a clean, airtight container.

To make the mocktail:

1. In a blender, place huckleberries or blueberries, splash of water, and the finely chopped needles of 1 sprig of rosemary. Blend until smooth and thick.
2. In a pourable 1-pint measuring cup or similar, stir sparkling water, rosemary simple syrup, lime juice, maple syrup, and skullcap tincture.
3. Add huckleberry mixture and stir.
4. Pour into two rocks glasses half filled with ice. Garnish with huckleberries or blueberries and a rosemary sprig. Sip and snuggle.

BROWN DEER

American Girl books avoid romance, except for the courtship of Kaya's sister, Brown Deer, by Cut Cheek, a young man from a neighboring tribe.

Courtship traditions vary across Indigenous cultures, and in some, like the Niimíipuu culture, avoiding direct eye contact has been a subtle way to express interest or respect. In the case of Brown Deer, she shows her interest in Cut Cheek by not looking at him! At a dance, boys signal their interest in a girl by laying a stick on her shoulder. Brown Deer shrugs off one boy's stick, but allows Cut Cheek's stick to stay, and they dance next to each other. Do they then exchange looks and smile? No, of course not. That's how you know they're in love.

Carpeted Cannonball

CAROLINE ABBOTT,
Historical Character 1812

**MAKES 1 DRINK/
COCKTAILS AND MOCKTAILS**

The hot toddy became popular in the United States by the early nineteenth century. This twist on the classic nightcap combines applejack brandy, bitters, and apples like the ones grown in orchards near Caroline's home turf—Sackets Harbor in Upstate New York.

INGREDIENTS

Honey syrup

½ cup water

½ cup honey

Cocktail

2 ounces apple cider

1 ounce honey syrup

2 ounces applejack brandy

½ ounce lemon juice, freshly squeezed

A few dashes of Angostura bitters

A pinch of ground cinnamon

A pinch of ground nutmeg

A splash of hot water, for dilution, if desired

Cinnamon stick, for garnish

Thin apple slice, for garnish

RECIPE STEPS

To make the honey syrup:

1. In a small saucepan over medium heat, heat water and honey. Stir lightly until dissolved.

2. Remove from heat and set aside to cool. There will be more than needed, so store the leftover in the refrigerator for up to two weeks.

To make the cocktail:

1. In a small saucepan, combine apple cider and honey syrup. Heat gently over medium to warm the mixture but do not boil.

2. Pour the mixture into a mug. Add applejack brandy, lemon juice, and bitters. Stir.

3. Sprinkle in cinnamon and nutmeg and stir again. If you'd like, add hot water for dilution.

4. Pop in a cinnamon stick for added flavor and aroma and as an appealing garnish. Hang a thin apple slice on the rim for an additional garnish. Serve immediately while warm. Savor the history with every sip!

CAROLINE ABBOTT

As the daughter of a shipbuilder with a thriving business, Caroline Abbott hopes to be a captain of her own ship one day. As a girl, she could choose to sit on the sidelines when the War of 1812 shows up on her front doorstep—but that's not in her nature. The British have already taken her father as a prisoner of war, and now they want her city and her father's shipyard. Her long-awaited bedroom carpet was just delivered, and she realizes the finery could serve a greater purpose. Bureaucratic bumbling has left the village vulnerable: Sackets Harbor can protect itself with cannons, but the shipment of cannonballs is too small. Where there is a problem, there is always a solution! Caroline relinquishes her brand-new rug to roll up inside the cannon, padding the rounds to make a cozy fit for firing. It works, and they blast the British, keeping them at bay, in the bay.

Friendship Brew

KIT KITTREDGE,
Historical Character 1934

MAKES 1 DRINK/
COCKTAILS AND MOCKTAILS

This brew is a nod to the stew Kit discovered when she visited the makeshift encampments adjacent to railroads where train hoppers wait for an outbound train. Everyone contributed something to the pot to make a meal for all. This hearty drink combines disparate ingredients that blend surprisingly well: Irish stout, amaretto from Italy, and Kentucky bourbon. Topped with Coca-Cola, this drink tastes like a grown-up root beer. Cheers to Kit!

INGREDIENTS

1 ounce amaretto
1 ounce coffee liqueur
1 ounce bourbon
3 ounces Irish stout or dark ale
3 ounces cola

RECIPE STEPS

1. Pour amaretto, coffee liqueur, and bourbon into a mixing glass. Stir and set aside.
2. In a wine glass (because this concoction is lowbrow but is overcoming its limitations), pour stout and cola.
3. Add in the amaretto mixture and stir. Taste the adventure!

KIT KITTREDGE

Before Kit Kittredge's father loses his job, she romanticizes a life without middle-class comforts. She is fascinated by the adventures of Robin Hood, living in Sherwood Forest, seeking justice for the downtrodden and poor. This resonates when she meets Will, an upbeat young man of integrity who is without a home, a job, or a family. During the Depression, some two million Americans were without homes. Young men like Will sometimes felt they were burdens on their strapped families and left home in search of work. However, ten-year-old Kit sees Will's life as a drifter as rich with adventure. After visiting the encampment where Will lives, she insists on riding the rails over his protests—and she and Will are arrested!

Disco Sour

JULIE ALBRIGHT,
Historical Character 1974

MAKES 1 DRINK/
COCKTAILS AND MOCKTAILS

San Francisco was one of the country's coolest disco scenes for dancing queens. Dressing Julie in funky threads, like a lemon-yellow crocheted vest and bell-bottom blue jeans with a fun flower pattern insert on each leg, she—and we—could move to the groove while playing the *Disco Dance Party* 45 on her working record player accessory. And her rotating mirrored disco ball let us all feel like "Hot Stuff"!

INGREDIENTS

Lime juice, for rim

Edible gold glitter, for rim and for sprinkling

2 ounces pisco

1 ounce Midori

½ ounce lime juice, freshly squeezed

½ ounce simple syrup

Club soda (optional)

RECIPE STEPS

1. Rim half of the edge of a coupe glass with lime juice and dip it into gold edible glitter. (It's fine to rim the whole glass, but since edible glitter doesn't have a taste, the texture on your lips can feel odd.)

2. In a cocktail shaker, combine pisco, Midori, lime juice, simple syrup, and two or three shakes of edible glitter. Dry shake (no ice).

3. Add ice and shake again until cold.

4. Strain into glitter-rimmed glass. The gold glitter should dance in the green drink.

5. To get glitter moving more, top with club soda. This step isn't necessary and will soften the taste of the cocktail.

6. Sprinkle more edible glitter on top. Sip and sparkle!

JULIE ALBRIGHT

Relaxing in her orange-upholstered egg chair that plays her favorite tunes in stereo, Historical Character Julie Albright is feeling groovy. Her room is filled with bright colors and fun florals, a nod to the popular prints and designs of the '70s. Her mom fills their home with thrift store décor from the shop she opened on her own after her divorce, blazing a trail alongside a generation of women starting their own businesses.

Acknowledgments

Some of the things we've learned from the stories of American Girls: appreciate what you have, celebrate your accomplishments, and recognize those who've helped you along the way. Taking the note, I want to share that it was my honor to write *The Official American Girl Cookbook: Fancy Food and Cocktails for Grown-Up Fans*. The experience was incredibly fun and fulfilling for me, and I'm so grateful to have been given the opportunity. Thank you to Running Press's senior editor Cindy Sipala for looking at my unique background as an authority in family entertainment and advocate for female empowerment and the host of annual entertainment-themed parties to realize that I would be a good fit for this project. And a huge thank you to my editor Maria Rillo, a true American Girl fan, for guidance and sharing her own American Girl love and experiences with me.

The journey involved reading all the books of the Historical Characters and Girls of the Year, absorbing the adoration of this brand from podcasters, laughing at the AG memes on social media, enjoying the dedicated AG fan websites and the Reddit subthreads, and talking to as many grown-up AG girls as possible. (Pro tip: when meeting a woman forty or younger, mention American

Girl to generate instant goodwill and conversation.) My hope is that you'll feel how much fun I had pairing a doll with a recipe that fits her and her time period perfectly—some earnest and some cheeky.

Who am I? I'm an idea generator like Maryellen, an independent thinker like Felicity, a curious journalist like Kit, a limelight lover like Rebecca, and a protector of children like Samantha. But in my career, I'm like Josefina—I like to do work that allows me to spend time with my family, and this was the perfect project for us! Thank you to

- my wonderful husband, Andy Stabile, the best home chef I know, who worked with me on recipe creation and ran our home test kitchen;
- my hilarious son Cole McNamara, who is brilliant at helping me come up with clever names and dish tie-ins for the dolls;
- my spirited daughter Riley Roberts, my American Girl Café companion for the last fifteen years, who visited American Girl stores with me around the country to capture the experience of every American Girl fan, no matter where she lives;
- my kind and helpful son Tate Stabile, along with his friends Nolan and Ryder, who served as my team of taste testers;
- our family friend Christie Dishner, who introduced all of us to the joy of American Girl two decades ago and who, somehow, makes every member of our family feel she is their sister;
- my mother-in-law, Sally Stabile, a baker whose highly anticipated treat boxes are the highlight of the holidays and whose Salted Caramel Rice Krispie Bar recipe is so good it had to be shared with the world;
- my neighbor Dan Feller, a great girl dad and actual rocket scientist, who used his STEM acumen to create the best version of the Mexican Candy Shot that's ever been made;
- my many friends who happily tested recipes for me to make sure my instructions were clear; and

- my parents, John and Sue Walker, who sacrificed their creative passions as a radio announcer and an artist to get "real jobs" that "pay money" to raise me and my brother, Jeff, and give us a solid education. As a result, we've both found paths to creative fulfillment and success in our fields of interest.

Special thanks to my film historian friends Sloan De Forest and Jeremy Arnold, who encouraged me for years, provided advice on getting into publishing, and made important introductions.

Writing this book fits into my life experience on a much deeper level than I originally thought. In researching the evolution of the American Girl brand, I see and respect everything Pleasant Rowland and the Mattel Corporation are doing to encourage generations of girls to enjoy childhood, discover and employ positive character traits, forgive themselves for mistakes (it happens to the best of us!), and allow for self-discovery. I've been as equally mission driven in my career, giving voice to kids in the movies made for them through a website I created with my kids and raising awareness to how messages in entertainment and media shape our own identities and decisions through my work at Common Sense Media and '80s Movie Guide. With every bite and sip from the recipes in this book, I hope you are fondly reminded of who you were as a child and how the toy you loved helped you to become the wonderful person you are now. Cheers!

Index

About the Author

Tara McNamara is a journalist specializing in the intersection of entertainment and culture. Recognized as an authority on family films and female-driven storytelling, McNamara explores how entertainment shapes us as individuals, generations, and society at large. She is a film reviewer for Common Sense Media, editor-in-chief of 80sMovieGuide.com, and cohost of the *Hays Gaze* spotlight series on Turner Classic Movies. As chair of the Critics Choice Association's Women's Committee, McNamara leads the Seal of Female Empowerment in Entertainment (SOFEE) initiative, recognizing movies and television series that portray females with authenticity. At sixteen, she was the manager of a toy store, giving her deep insight into our emotional connection to childhood playthings—and a lifelong excuse to stay a kid at heart. She lives in Hermosa Beach, California, and hosts an annual Oscar party known for its outrageous nominee-inspired menu.